Contents

Preface

The early 1980s would seem an appropriate time to reflect on geographical education. The past decade has seen fundamental reforms in the nature and presentation of geography in secondary schools, and growing claims to professionalism on the part of geography teachers based on the curriculum theory used to justify such change. While the new geography has become a powerful orthodoxy, there are already growing signs of the subject's declining popularity amongst pupils and of school geography's increasing irrelevance to pressing social problems. A widening communication gap has developed between school and university geographers, and there is some indifference to the subject's claims on the part of those with control over the school curriculum. In addition many geography teachers are experiencing growing feelings of frustration and helplessness as pupils become more resistant, administrators more demanding, resources less generous, and parents and society more critical of their work. It is against such a background that this book seeks to provide geography teachers with a critical account of recent curriculum change and with pointers to emerging alternatives which may better serve personal and social needs. Its central thesis is that the new geography was a conservative and adaptive response to prevailing social realities and that subsequent developments in geography and education now allow geography teachers to make a more constructive contribution to human development and social justice.

I hope that the book will prompt reflection on recent curriculum change in school geography and encourage action on emerging possibilities which themselves involve reflection and action. In inviting contributions I approached those who I perceived to be sympathetic to its central message. While our diagnoses and prescriptions encompass a variety of beliefs, they stem from common commitments, and are offered in the hope that they will lead to a greater number of reflective and active geographers in our schools.

John Huckle
Bedford, January 1982

Introduction

The new or reformed geography, introduced into schools in the early 1970s, brought great changes in subject content, teaching and learning methods, and curriculum design and evaluation. Geography as science was seen by many as superior to a descriptive, factual geography, and its component concepts and ideas not only offered more logical and complete knowledge but were amenable to rational curriculum planning. Its methodology brought exciting new techniques and instructional possibilities, and the attendant need for mathematics changed the appearance of many textbooks and blackboards. New geography enabled many teachers to increase their use of enquiry-based methods and their move to more informal classrooms was encouraged by Schools Council projects and in-service education. Such agencies also prompted geography teachers to regard themselves as professionals with new roles and responsibilities, supported by new skills in curriculum development and implementation. By 1980 the new geography had become a powerful orthodoxy supported by new curriculum materials, new examination syllabuses, and key figures in the professional community. It was, however, meeting increasing criticism, as Chapters 1 and 2 suggest.

At the same time as the new geography was being introduced into schools, some academic geographers and curriculum theorists were beginning to express concern about the undue attention to science within their respective fields. Their discontent focused on the personal costs of rationalism as a style of thought, for they believed that studies of landscapes and schooling which stressed hard objectivity eroded people's sensitivity and stifled their development. In stressing humanism as an alternative to rationalism, they wished to acknowledge the aesthetic, ethical, and spiritual dimensions of human existence, and to develop alternative forms of geographical and curriculum theory based on different premises, procedures, and tests for truth.

The content of the new geography brought personal costs in that it asked teachers and pupils to suspend feelings, intuition, and imagination, and to regard human environments as mere exemplars of scientific facts and theories. It required them to discount private everyday experience and to think of themselves as insignificant inhabitants of a world in which truth and knowledge are static features of external reality, and they are victims of natural and social forces over which they have little control. In such circumstances human values and potentials are denied, and geography lessons lose much of their appeal. It is therefore not surprising that the new geography has proved unacceptable to some teachers, and its content, language, and technicalities have been blamed for the subject's declining popularity in schools.

Rex Beddis and Nicholas Helburn were key figures amongst those who reformed the geography curriculum on either side of the Atlantic and their contributions are designed to allow the reader to reflect on change in school geography since 1960. Rex Beddis contrasts the confident optimism of the 1960s with the reformist zeal of the 1970s and the uncertainty of the 1980s. He writes of personal doubts and mixed feelings concerning the new geography, and of those features of pupils, schools, and society which increasingly point to the relevance of curriculum developments outside geography. Aware of the growing constraints on radical curriculum reform, he nevertheless identifies some grounds for optimism in geography's renewed attention to place and politics.

Nicholas Helburn, who directed the American High School Geography Project in the 1960s, outlines the evolution of a style of curriculum development which was to have later parallels in Britain. He acknowledges that the geographers who worked with the project did have a strong commitment to science, but believes that certain of its activities should have served to counter the personal and social costs of the new geography and that curriculum developers generally handled the new geography's content and methodology in such a way as to ameliorate the worst excesses of hard objectivity. The enquiry-based learning proposed by curriculum projects required facts and theories to be given personal relevance and it had much potential to alleviate pupil discontent. Nicholas Helburn is, however, pessimistic about the widespread adoption of such approaches and considers that the conservative nature of schools and teachers ensures that much classroom geography fails to connect with pupils' lives.

If the proposed teaching and learning methods served to lessen the personal costs of changed content, the new geography's use of rational curriculum planning did serve to further alienate many teachers. A curriculum designed by experts using ideas which stressed efficiency, predictability, and control seemed to discount their own experience and intuitive responses to the needs of pupils, and to encourage a mechanistic approach to life in classrooms. Teachers often failed to recognize in rational curriculum theory any account of teaching, learning, or course planning which matched their everyday lives, and many were critical of its limited ability to accommodate those affective outcomes which they regarded as central to the process of education.

Humanistic geographical education

The alternative forms of geography, education, and curriculum studies which humanists developed in the 1970s sought to reveal the everyday meanings of environmental and educational phenomena which we use to make sense of our lives. Such meanings consist of inseparable facts and values and are socially constructed through being largely shared with others. Quiet attentiveness to environmental and educational encounters can reveal the meanings which places, lessons, and curricula have for participants, and can also aid the self-awareness of the observer. While humanistic geographers explore people's private geographies and their emotional attachment to place, humanistic educators also seek to acknowledge feelings, interests, and concerns. Their lessons encourage pupils to clarify values, balance facts and feelings, and acquire a sense of their own identity and moral growth. Humanistic curriculum studies recognizes the relativity of school knowledge, seeks to preserve teachers and pupils as meaning-makers, and attempts to reveal the processes whereby such phenomena as the new geography become realities in teachers' lives.

John Fien and Frances Slater write in Chapters 3 and 4 of the possibilities which behavioural geography and humanistic geography offer to teachers wishing to counter the personal costs of the new geography. With its emphasis on perception, behavioural geography deals with those mental images of the world which shape our environmental attitudes and behaviour. It accommodates personal and evaluative knowledge, but remains a reformist response to the excesses of the new geography since it continues to draw on science and to regard perception as a mere barrier to rational decision-making and behaviour. Humanistic geography is more interested in our everyday experience and meanings of place for their own sake, and is not prepared to separate knowledge and values. John Fien shows how it allows teachers to give greater attention to pupils' private geographies and so fosters their self-awareness and environmental competence. Coupled with the experiential learning methods of humanistic or confluent education, it provides a convincing new rationale for geography within the humanities.

In Chapter 5 Eric Brough suggests that art as an expression of human sensitivity to the environment deserves greater attention in geography classrooms. Painters, writers, and musicians strive to express the significance of human encounters with landscape, and by cultivating aesthetic awareness we can allow our pupils to glimpse the lasting truths underlying the human predicament. Art is perhaps as central to humanistic geographical education as mathematics was to the new geography. Many teachers disenchanted with rationalism will welcome the opportunities it offers.

Radical geographical education

While humanists rejected the new geography on behalf of the individual, the radical geographers and curriculum theorists who emerged in the mid 1970s denied its value on behalf of the community. They suggested that dominant forms of geography and education were not making a relevant contribution to social problems and could be seen to be distracting attention away from the true causes of growing injustice. They perceived a widening gap between the claims made on behalf of science and technology and their practical success when applied to the control and management of our lives. Some academic geographers therefore questioned the social relevance and political neutrality of their work, and engaged in attempts to adapt their new scientific theories and methods to genuine issues of human welfare. A comparable response in curriculum studies was to seek relevance in terms of the integrated curriculum. Such recipes as environmental or social studies were often seized upon by geography teachers who claimed that the abstractions and technicalities of the new geography were irrelevant to their pupils' future lives.

A more profound criticism of the new geography was that it constituted a form of social control serving to maintain exploitative relationships within our advanced capitalist society. Its ideas were seen as ideology which supported the interests of those with wealth and power by encouraging people to accept the status quo. While appearing to explain and justify existing social conditions, the ideas concealed the true nature of social and human-environment relationships and the real causes of worsening social problems. By questioning the assumed neutrality of those geographical theories and techniques which were being applied to the management and control of society, radicals encouraged fellow academics to adopt a more open and committed approach to their political role in society. They rediscovered radical geographies based on Marxism and anarchism and used these both to reinterpret the recent history of the subject, and to provide a genuinely critical geography which seeks to transform existing social conditions through both theory and action.

If much academic geography had become ideology posing as science, the same was true of geography in schools. Radical curriculum theorists suggested that such developments as the new geography encourage a conservative perspective on society and condition pupils for their future lives in a technocratic state. When taught without reference to their social and historical origins, or the interests they serve, certain of its ideas and techniques foster an uncritical view of the world. Their ideological role is reinforced by enquiry-based learning which encourages pupils to test hypotheses, solve problems, and make decisions only within the narrow confines of given geographical theories and political options. Radicals were also critical of the rational curriculum theory used to support the new geography in schools. By stressing means rather than ends, and presenting teachers with ready-made curriculum packages, the new curriculum experts were effectively stifling genuine debate on the ideal form of school geography, and at the same time de-skilling teachers by reducing them to technicians. The content, teaching methods, and curriculum rationale of the new geography all contained strong elements of social control.

The alternative forms of education and curriculum theory which radicals proposed were based on the desire to make schooling an agent of cultural criticism and social reconstruction, rather than one of social reproduction. Once alert to the role of the curriculum in sustaining 'appropriate' beliefs and work habits, it was not sufficient merely to seek relevance through the merging of subjects in integrative frameworks. Ideas could continue to act as ideology whether taught in geography or integrated studies, and the true need was for forms of education which fostered critical awareness and continually tested the relevance of knowledge in real or simulated action. A radical curriculum based on this premise removes pupils' feelings of political powerlessness and facilitates both decisions and actions on social issues, particularly those affecting the local community. It requires an open and considered approach to social conflict and politics in schools which allows teachers to defend themselves against the frequent charges of indoctrination which radicals face.

In Chapter 6 John Bale describes how welfare geographers modified the theories and techniques of the new geography to incorporate a concern for human well-being. He shows how their descriptions, explanations, and predictions of spatial inequalities may be introduced in the classroom, and concludes that these are likely to be more acceptable to schools and teachers than those of radical geography. While Ian Cook would support this contention, he introduces the limitations of a reformist approach in Chapter 7. Since dominant forms of academic and school geography are the products of an unjust material reality, committed geographers and teachers should seek to erode the hold of ideology with alternative ideas and actions. His analysis of *People, Place and Work* from the Avery Hill 14–16 Project not only illustrates ideological bias in school geography, but suggests alternative approaches for teaching about the world of work. The teacher implementing these could face opposition and is likely to require the defences which a greater understanding of political education can offer. My own short introduction to political education in schools in Chapter 8 argues that the approach based on political literacy can accommodate geographical ideas from a variety of ideological contexts. By developing appropriate knowledge, skills, and attitudes, teachers can encourage political autonomy and foster a critical approach to geographical knowledge. This strategy is illustrated by a discussion of environmental management and nuclear power, both topics with much potential for political education.

Chapters 9, 10 and 11 describe attempts to provide a relevant curriculum via development education, environmental education, and urban studies. David Hicks urges geography teachers to give greater attention to the related issues of development, minority rights, and race. He explains how changed thinking about development and development education has prompted a greater sensitivity to stereotyping, racist attitudes, and bias in the curriculum, and has led to a more open approach to colonialism, neo-colonialism, and racism in the classroom. In order to contribute to development at personal, local, national, and global levels geography teachers should acknowledge the needs of minorities and their subject's considerable potential in the field of multi-ethnic education. Case studies of the poor and oppressed overseas should be supplemented by a consideration of poverty and oppression both in Britain and the local neighbourhood. Chapter 9 shows that the materials and teaching methods to support such lessons are now available and await wider discovery.

The conservative, liberal, and radical ideologies which prompt varied approaches to development education also find expression in environmental education. In Chapter 10 I suggest that the dominant forms of environmental studies in schools serve to conceal the true nature of the environmental crisis and so sustain deterioration in environmental quality. Radical environmental education, with its attention to moral and political outcomes, now has a considerable literature, but has not gained wide support amongst geography teachers. It requires a more open and critical approach to those social conflicts in which the environment functions as an instrument of human exploitation, and is likely to lead pupils and teachers towards the type of involvement in local issues which Chris Webb describes in Chapter 11. At Notting Dale Urban Studies Centre he has pioneered community-based approaches to environmental education which encourage people to reflect on their circumstances and develop the political skills necessary to use, control, and change their surroundings. He gives examples of such projects and suggests that they have far-reaching implications for conventional schools. If such schools are to remain relevant to the lives and aspirations of the majority of their pupils, they will need to adopt a more open curriculum, base local study on real involvement, and be more ready to confront bureaucracy on behalf of the underpriviledged. Changes in these directions could lead to a truly radical and integrated curriculum in which geography is a mere resource providing some of the ideas and methods by which pupils can help to transform their world.

Geography in the 1980s

The final three chapters provide geography teachers sympathetic to its earlier messages with advice on facing the future. Robin Richardson deals with the personal and professional competences required by humanistic and radical teachers, while Michael Storm reminds us of the material circumstances in which their idealism and commitment are likely to be strongly tested. In the last chapter I attempt an interpretation of the political role of the new geography in schools and seek to summarize the emerging possibilities whereby geography teachers may now make a constructive response to social change.

Robin Richardson outlines the related techniques, skills, and values and attitudes which will best serve the needs of those who 'dare to be teachers'. He stresses the importance of structured discussion in classrooms and in courses for teachers, and explains how the moral culture which it can foster leads to greater sensitivity, more respect for others, and a stronger commitment to social justice. As teachers try the techniques he suggests, acquire new skills, and clarify their values and attitudes, they will become more self-confident and more competent in the political skills required within the school and community. In short, they will become capable of translating into action the theoretical understandings outlined elsewhere in the book.

In discussing likely curriculum trends in the 1980s, Michael Storm puts the emphasis on the 'dull and gritty management problems' we will have to face. Reinforcing Rex Beddis's earlier remarks, he reminds us that while the new geography evolved in a climate of growth and optimism, school geography in the 1980s must adapt to the very different world of falling rolls, public spending cuts, accountability, and increased scepticism on the part of both pupils and the public. The political skills mentioned by Robin Richardson will be tested to the full, but Michael Storm suggests that good could come from adversity. Falling rolls may encourage mixed-ability teaching and common systems of examining, a reduction of curriculum choice may require geographers to incorporate such new concerns as political and development education, less money for duplicating worksheets may lead to more enlightened teaching, and more non-specialists may provoke greater attention to the monitoring of curriculum structure and progression. Provided we are prepared to remedy the costs of the trickle down curriculum development of the 1970s and adopt a more socially responsive definition of teacher professionalism, Michael Storm believes that geography can maintain its present status in schools. Its greatest asset is its ability to deal with such areas of broad popular concern as environmental and international understanding. Despite the ominous tone of some pronouncements on the secondary curriculum, a more humanistic and radical form of school geography could be with us for a long time to come.

In extending and qualifying the arguments I have made about the new geography in this introduction, the final chapter assesses the degree of correspondence between school geography and the manpower and socialization needs of society. It places recent developments in school geography in the context of wider political debates about the nature and purpose of education and is critical of the social democratic consensus underlying so many of the curriculum proposals made by geographers. In advocating an alternative socialist approach to school geography, the chapter recognizes growing potential for the approaches suggested elsewhere in this book and forecasts a period of conflict as geography teachers come to terms with their inevitably political role.

Section A **Retrospect**

'. . . the essentially methodological revolution of locational analysis which did not involve a fundamental questioning of philosophy led to change at the frontier of higher education and to the passing of "instructions" down the educational hierarchy and so to the consequent distortion rather than the replacement of orthodox geography.'
Roger Lee, 1977

'. . . a society of puppets with no dreams to dream and nothing to be sorry for. Instead of implementing plans which will aid man in his striving for becoming, we get entangled in descriptive, objective, and analytic techniques, which will produce just the opposite. Instead of building a world for the constant groping of autonomous man, we are confining ourselves within spatial and social prisons which will serve only to increase our sense of loss and futility. Instead of preserving ambiguity, we impose certainty.'
Gunnar Olsson, 1975

'This so-called revolution (the new geography) was, in fact, profoundly conservative as it reified the spatial as the subject of the discipline. At the same time it diverted attention away from the underlying structural explanations of society and economy, as part of a general process of "mystification" whereby surface manifestations are confused for root causes.'
David Smith and Philip Ogden, 1977

'What must be of concern to all geographers is that without continued discussion and debate institutional inertia will force school geography to reach a *modus vivendi* with quantification and positivism only in the 1990s and that if this does happen it will represent a lost decade.'
Peter Newby, 1980

Chapter 1

Geographical education since 1960: a personal view

Rex Beddis

Reflecting on the past can be a fairly harmless form of self-indulgence, involving little more than a range of pleasures and regrets. On the other hand, it can afford a perspective on events that was impossible during the time itself. Perhaps it may provide a deeper understanding of what happened and of the nature of change. The following is a personal account of events related to geographical education since 1960. It is subjective and idiosyncratic, and bound to differ from the experiences and perceptions of colleagues in different institutions and other parts of the country. It describes a period in which my reactions to curriculum developments have ranged from the resistant to the accepting, the anxious to the confident—often, it seemed, all at the same time.

At the beginning of the 1960s I was a classroom teacher and head of geography with six years' experience of teaching in two large purpose-built comprehensive schools in inner London. By the early 1970s my role had changed to that of co-director of a Schools Council geography project following five years as a lecturer in a college of education with a lively and vigorous geography department. In the early 1980s my role had changed yet again to that of a local education authority adviser with responsibility for the humanities area of the curriculum in some five hundred primary and secondary schools. Even if there had been no significant external pressure for change, these role variations would undoubtedly have led to changes in my thinking about the aims, content, and methodology of geographical education.

In fact, substantial and rapid change has been one of the dominant characteristics of the period—in society as a whole, in the educational system, in geography as an academic subject, and in geographical education at school level. It is a truism that people respond to change in different ways. Some resist external pressures to the bitter end, and only change in a superficial manner when forced to do so. Others accept the need for change, but do so with great caution and anxiety. Yet others seem to regard change as a vital ingredient in their work, and if it is not imposed on them will generate it themselves. Most people exhibit elements of all these responses to varying degrees, depending on their abilities, circumstances, support provided by colleagues and institutions, and their attitude to continuity and change.

The move to realism

The early 1960s was a good time to be teaching geography in inner London. Many purpose-built comprehensive schools had been opened in the previous decade, and geography departments seemed to have been favoured by the architects. A usual arrangement was for two or three large, carefully designed and well-equipped rooms to be located at the top of the main building—in some cases with superb views over the London skyline. Duplicating facilities and audio-visual equipment were available for the exclusive use of the department—not TV, video recorders or offset litho, admittedly, but all sorts of projectors and the invaluable 'Banda'. There was plenty of storage space and large working and display areas. There must have been some limits to capitation, but there never seemed any shortage of consumable materials, nor desperate need for more maps, atlases or textbooks. The working environment was more than adequate.

As far as teaching staff went, there was a good balance of those with experience gained in pre-comprehensive days and newcomers to the profession, all of whom had chosen to work in London in this particular kind of school. The school-leaving age had not then been raised to sixteen, and while there were certainly truculent and aggressive pupils and very difficult classes, the general mood amongst staff and pupils was one of enjoyment, challenge, and optimism. A new experiment in school organization was being tried, and while it was not without teething troubles, there was every expectation that things would improve with time and experience.

Apart from the favourable physical environment and the stimulus of able and enthusiastic colleagues, there was also a mood of optimism and a sense of development in the world of geographical education—at least in the London area. A desultory year in the School of Education in one of our older universities had done absolutely nothing to prepare me for the practical job of teaching geography in a comprehensive school. It is now possible to see the considerable influence of the geography department of the University of London Institute of Education on geography teachers in the London area during that period.

One of the biggest influences on, and supports for, geography teachers in the early 1960s was the textbook series *Geography for Schools* (ed. Honeybone, 1958), written largely by geographers at the Institute. These textbooks put into practical form the ideas expressed so clearly and eloquently in *Geography and Education*, the Ministry of Education pamphlet published in 1960. Together, the series and pamphlet gave the theoretical and practical guidelines for geographical education in the early 1960s.

A main aim at that time seemed to be the replacement of rote learning of abstract and highly generalized descriptive information, presented in a regional framework, with an awareness and understanding of what places, people, and the relationships between them were actually like. A greater variety of resources were becoming available—filmstrips, slides, films, radio programmes, and sample studies, for example. Some twenty years earlier the textbook series *Real Geography* (Fairgreave and Young, 1939) had suggested what might be done. The post-war improvement in the design and production of books meant that more photographs, diagrams, and maps could be used. Case or sample studies became popular both in such textbook series as *A Course in World Geography* (Young and Lowry, 1960), and in such collections as *Sample Studies* (Geographical Association, 1962) and *Study Geography* (Rushby, Bell and Dybeck, 1967). Realism was a key aim, and resources were being provided to help young people gain some idea of what places and life styles were like.

Another manifestation of this striving for realism was the growth of fieldwork which sought to make the real world accessible to pupils. This led to larger-scale studies than the more traditional regions of textbooks, and encouraged rather different techniques and study methods. Inner London Education Authority teachers were offered many in-service courses on field-work areas and methods owing to the interest and enthusiasm of the staff inspector, Miss M. Goss. She had been a co-author of one of the books in the *Geography for Schools* series, and was a staunch supporter of the London Institute approach. Fieldwork, albeit in the form of excursions, descriptive walks, and fairly indiscriminate recording of data, became more widely practised. A number of handbooks were published, a significant one being *Fieldwork in Geography* (Archer and Dalton, 1968). Fieldwork was positively encouraged by the requirements of the newly developed Metropolitan CSE syllabus and examination. It is interesting to recall the influence and power of the ILEA staff inspector, various members of the London Institute, and authors such as Archer and Dalton on the CSE geography panel. Even at this stage, though, fieldwork was still predominantly rural or suburban, and tended to be based on day trips or residential courses in the countryside.

In retrospect the London geography scene of the early 1960s appears somewhat introverted, with initial training, in-service training, textbook provision, CSE geography panel decisions and local Geographical Associ-ation activities being dominated by an interrelated and supportive group of geographers. Being in sympathy with the aims of the group, I felt part of a vigorous, self-confident, and developing movement. A good impression of the strength of the network can be gained from the London Institute *Hand-book for Geography Teachers* (ed. Long, 1964), while the philosophy and methodology advocated by the Institute is clearly expressed in *Teaching Geography* (Long and Roberson, 1966). Other attitudes and practices might be found elsewhere, but they in no way challenged the supremacy of the 'London school'. The International Geographical Union Congress of 1964 was held in London with a symposium on geographical education taking place at Goldsmiths College. Even there a key figure was the Canadian professor, Neville Scarfe, himself an ex-London Institute man. There were other well-known centres of geographical education such as Sheffield and Bristol, but these appeared as outposts preaching the same message as the metropolis, rather than places where revolution was being fostered. This was indeed the case. When the revolution came, it came from other, quite unexpected, directions.

A search for theory

The decade between 1960 and 1970 has acquired the popular label of the 'swinging sixties'. Whatever the term really means, there is no doubt that it was a time of considerable change in general attitudes and social behaviour. In its own small way the geographical world also experienced a revolution, and its impact on school geography can be traced back to a series of courses for teachers held at Madingley in Cambridgeshire. Many younger geographers in British universities were interpreting and developing approaches already established in North America and Scandinavia, but the two who seem to have had the greatest impact on the teaching profession were Richard Chorley and Peter Haggett. These were the names most readily associated with the new geography. Indeed one antagonistic professor of geography coined the word 'Haggettry' as a word of contempt for the new movement.

Relatively few geography teachers had direct experience of these new ideas through the Madingley lectures, and the first significant dissemination (a word rarely used in those days) took place one Saturday in the late 1960s at Haberdashers' Aske's School, Elstree. The meeting had been called by Brian FitzGerald and John Everson, both geography teachers in independent schools who were early disciples of the so-called new geography. The aim was to discuss the weakness of the idiographic approach and the need to change to a nomothetic one. These words, when checked in the dictionary, certainly conveyed a confusing and provocative message. In the event an unexpectedly large audience of curious people turned up, and the movement was launched.

The earliest books elaborating this new movement were *Frontiers in Geographical Teaching* (eds. Chorley and Haggett, 1965), *Locational Analysis in Human Geography* (Haggett, 1965) and *Models in Geography* (eds. Chorley and Haggett, 1967). These books led to a mixture of excitement and confusion, and to extremes of response from the teaching profession. They were more difficult to understand and accept than the rather earlier *Statistical Methods for the Geographer* (Gregory, 1963), for even if this was difficult to understand and use, at least one could see its relevance to geography teaching. It is worth noting that these publications are of about the same date as Long and Roberson's powerful defence of the idiographic approach in *Teaching Geography*. The work of the American High School Geography Project began to be disseminated in this country in the middle 1960s, and the very significant (for the participants if for no one else) first Charney Manor conference was held in the spring of 1970. A flavour of the excitement and enthusiasm of this conference can be gained from the papers published in book form as *New Directions in Geography Teaching* (ed. Walford, 1973). The groundwork for the major change of emphasis in school geography was completed with the publication of *Games in Geography* (Walford, 1973). If Chorley and Haggett appeared as the academics leading the new geography, Everson, FitzGerald, and Walford were the names that were associated with its introduction into schools.

The new geography

In the early 1970s, then, the enlightened traditionalism of the early 1960s had been challenged and a fundamentally different approach to geographical education proposed. It took most teachers some time to appreciate that the introduction of statistical methods was not the heart of the matter, and that the main difference was in the emphasis on theory, particularly that relating to spatial patterns and processes. Attempts were made to develop spatial concepts into various sorts of models, while an appropriate mode of enquiry was encouraged—that of hypothesis generation and testing. This stress on theories and models implied that geography was less interested in the unique case—the particular farm, town, region—than in generalizations. Areal differentiation was no longer seen to be a concept of importance, and regional geography of the old descriptive style fell into disrepute. The study of space, the geometry of landscape and society, became more important than the study of real and specific cases unrelated to theory.

Alongside this change was an increased emphasis on understanding, rather than factual learning, as an aim of education. It is only fair to comment that the best of the more traditional geography, even with its concern for the unique, was just as critical of unthinking rote learning, and just as supportive of an understanding that could be transferred to new situations. It was also argued that theoretical geography could quite easily become little more than rote learning, even if concepts and models did replace mere descriptive facts. There is no question, though, that the emphasis of the new movement was on the generation and understanding of ideas.

It was probably easier for me to think through these new ideas and implement them while teaching in a college of education than in the more demanding atmosphere of an ordinary classroom. Colleges of education had experienced remarkable growth during the 1960s, and in many geography departments there were people with the ability and time to assist in the difficult task of translating proposals into practice. On a personal level it had not been an easy adaptation. The invitation to the Haberdashers' Aske's day conference had produced a mixture of suspicion and confusion, and the event itself proved so threatening to the established order that my first reaction was one of resistance and counter-challenge. (A hurriedly written article challenging the movement was fortunately rejected by the editor of *Geography*!) It took much patient explanation during dozens of meetings and conferences (the innovators remained remarkably calm and polite in the face of some extreme hostility and arrogant contempt from many of the established school), together with many articles, books and informal discussions before I could accept the main principles. Without any doubt the key event in my conversion was the Charney Manor conference in 1970. I still had many uncertainties and doubts about new trends, but from that weekend onwards I felt part of a group of like-minded enthusiasts who were doing more than jumping on a bandwagon. From then on it became a matter of working on the details and implementing ideas at the classroom level.

While this upheaval was taking place in the world of geographical education, changes of considerable importance were occurring in the wider educational system and in society at large. The school-leaving age had been raised to sixteen years, and reluctant pupils were challenging many traditional attitudes. One response had been the establishment of a number of

Schools Council young school leaver projects to try to identify a curriculum suitable for older, less able pupils in the schools of the 1970s. The geographical profession was well represented on Schools Council committees, and as a result a geography project was launched in 1970 to support teachers working with these less able and frequently poorly motivated youngsters. It cannot be too strongly emphasized that the Geography for the Young School Leaver Project (GYSL) was motivated by a concern for the curricular needs of lower ability pupils, and their teachers, rather than a wish to implement the new geography that was being promulgated.

The fact that the Geography 14–18 (Bristol) Project was funded at the same time to support work with more able pupils of the same age was less a result of rational planning than of disagreement between geographical educators about priorities, and of the internal politics of various committees. Several members of the two project central teams were personal friends, and in the early days efforts were consciously made to exchange views and work together. In practice, though, little liaison or collaboration took place, and there was a tacit agreement to go their different ways. Fundamental differences can, in retrospect, be related to contrasting attitudes to both geographical education and curriculum development. Geography 14–18 based its proposals on a theoretical analysis of the discipline whereas GYSL started with a consideration of the needs and wants of young people, and then attempted to seek a relevant contribution from the discipline. In terms of curriculum development Geography 14–18 placed great emphasis on the professional ability of teachers to develop their own curriculum, whereas GYSL had a more pragmatic approach to the problems of classroom innovation and curriculum change. These differences were partly attributable to different 'consumers' and partly to the different attitudes and experiences of the team members. It is only now that the differences are beginning to blur. Teachers associate themselves with both projects, teach pupils of all abilities, and enter candidates for GCE O level and CSE. Both projects have in effect practised a three-fold strategy of providing resources and guides, establishing collaborative teacher groups, and becoming partners in examination systems. It is impossible to know the harmful consequences of having two projects running at the same time in this way, but perhaps the very existence of an alternative project, with which the other would inevitably be compared, provided a stimulus that sharpened the performance of both.

Whatever the motives that led to the two projects being funded, by the time of their launch in 1970 the central team members were well aware of the changes in geography being advocated by the group of innovators referred to above. The project teams had the difficult task of both absorbing and understanding such change while at the same time judging its relevance to school geography and acting as agents in disseminating what was felt to be worthwhile. It is for others to decide how well the teams managed to reflect the new geography in forms acceptable to pupils and teachers during the 1970s. It would be foolish to exaggerate the effect of the Schools Council geography projects on geographical education as a whole, but there is little doubt that they were a significant and probably the dominant influence on

15

geography teaching in secondary schools in the middle and late 1970s. This was seen not only in the widespread use of project resources and project-related examinations, but also in the thinking behind new courses and examinations in many boards, and more latterly in new textbook series.

The four years I worked with the Schools Council GYSL Project proved a remarkable experience, quite unlike any other within geographical education. The luxury of working nationally with professional educators, translating their experience and provocative new ideas into a worthwhile curriculum for young people, was a rare privilege. The time was just right in the sense that there was an obvious demand for ideas and resources. Geography teachers and their pupils wanted something more relevant and interesting than the traditional watered-down academic course or the trivial topic. It was also right in that this was about the most optimistic time for curriculum development as a creative activity permeating the whole education system. Relatively large amounts of money were available, local authorities were able and willing to support in-service education, and there was a belief in collaboration at the local level between teachers, lecturers, and advisers in curriculum design and development.

Some teachers remained unwilling to concede the desirability of a conceptual geography, perhaps more than one would like to admit. It is also true that, taken as a whole, pupils were becoming more truculent and challenging to authority. In some schools teaching was proving a very demanding and almost overwhelming job. Nevertheless there was a widespread mood of optimism. The geographical world seemed to have weathered reasonably well the storms of a changed geography, the raising of the school-leaving age, and the pressures for a curriculum relevant to the needs of the decade. Geographers could with some justification congratulate themselves that their contribution to the school curriculum was as vigorous, up-to-date, and progressive as that of any other discipline.

A relevant geography for a changing world

The enthusiasm, optimism, and confidence of the early and mid 1970s are much harder to discover today. Undoubtedly this is a reflection of a much wider malaise, both national and global. On the global scale the gap between rich and poor nations seems to be getting wider; there are signs of environmental damage being wilfully pursued for economic gains; populations are growing and urbanization proceeding at a near disastrous pace; and international relations are precarious, to say the least. A period of severe economic recession has produced high inflation and severe unemployment in many countries of the world, including the so-called developed nations of Western Europe and North America. At the national scale the educational system has had to take its share of cuts as well as being obliged to cope with declining rolls. Geography teachers, along with others, have to work in an atmosphere of uncertainty, real reduction in resource backing, and confusion about their role in a changing society where near certainty of unemployment faces many of their pupils, no matter how industrious or able.

Geography teachers feel additionally threatened by the apparent, though disclaimed, low status afforded the subject in several important Department of Education and Science and Her Majesty's Inspectorate documents. In spite of their support for a curriculum which would 'help young people understand the world in which they live', geography appears not to be recognized as a significant element of the core curriculum. Some have gone so far as to say that if choices have to be made, it would be better for pupils to study history rather than geography. It is impossible to judge how significant these opinions will be in determining the status of geography in schools in the 1980s. What is obvious is that the confident assertions and claims made about the subject by geographers are not universally accepted. This may be because such claims more often state what might, rather than what actually does happen. On the other hand, it could be that even the well-designed and implemented geography course has little credibility for most pupils and adults. It has to be faced that many pupils, parents, employers and professionals other than geographers would themselves be quite unmoved if geography disappeared from the curriculum.

If geography is to survive as a genuinely worthwhile subject, enjoyed and valued by pupils and adults, it will have to adjust to the needs of the 1980s. There are a few pointers as to the directions these changes might take. One of the consequences of being responsible for the humanities area of the curriculum is the contact it brings with a wide range of professionals other than geographers. There is no question that working with planners, architects, artists, economists, community workers and so on is enormously stimulating and challenging to dearly held beliefs. As a geographer it is difficult not to be impressed and influenced by people involved in projects such as Art and the Built Environment, or in various political education activities, or engaged in community action from bases such as Notting Dale Urban Studies Centre. The environmental, political, aesthetic, multi-cultural, development and economic education movements all seem to have a vitality and relevance lacking in many geography syllabuses.

Criticism of existing practice is easier to accept if accompanied by alternative proposals. A personal view is that while geographical education needs to be self-critical, there are several ways in which it could now adjust in order to become a more worthwhile subject for young people in the 1980s. Firstly, there is a need to re-establish an interest in and concern for place, since an awareness and enjoyment of the variety of place is a fundamental human characteristic. So much travel, literature, art, music, and journalism is rooted in this fact, and some would argue that it is the growth of similar environments and the monotony of placelessness that is a major cause of much contemporary dissatisfaction. One only has to read novels such as *The Alexandria Quartet* (Durrell, 1960), travel writings such as *Destinations* (Morris, 1981), philosophical works such as *Topophilia* (Tuan, 1974) or to look at landscapes by any one of hundreds of artists from all ages and parts of the world to be convinced of the significance and richness of places for most people. Undoubtedly there is a need for theorizing and modelling real places into abstract forms, but it seems perverse and almost intellectually snobbish

17

to reject the chance of offering youngsters the additional pleasure of 'sensing' different places around the world.

Secondly, the explanations offered by geographers need to be more catholic and honest. In this respect geographers have much to learn from the political and development education movements. If geography teachers really want to help young people understand the world in which they live, they will need to explain not just the landscape, but the total social, economic, and political life in places. One has to concede that such explanations may be complex, and difficult to simplify for young people, but honest explanations of patterns and processes often demand economic, social, or political understanding. This, incidentally, is as true at local and regional scales as at the national and international.

There could be lengthy debate about the major issues facing society, but some stand out as quite fundamental. Most would include urbanization, resource depletion, environmental destruction, population growth, disparities in living standards, and the exploitation of some people by others. Many of these issues have a moral component, and it is hard to see how one can, or should want to, introduce young people to them on a purely intellectual or explanatory level. They matter not only to millions of individual people but to the future well-being of the whole human race. A geography worth including in a school curriculum should take its share of responsibility for helping young people explore their attitudes towards these complex issues. Some might be painful to consider—unemployment, or inadequate housing, for example—but at least they may help pupils realize and understand their own situation. That, surely, is an important function of true education. There is a danger that a largely conceptual geography in schools could be intellectually challenging, but colourless and morally sterile. It is easy to see how books such as *Beginning the New Geography* (Briggs, 1969) and *Human Geography* (Bradford and Kent, 1977), admirable as they are in their own terms, could lead to a geography without feeling or compassion. Perhaps this is the price of emphasizing the objectivity of geography as a social science rather than its subjectivity as a humanities discipline. The attempt to reconcile these different approaches may be the major challenge for geography teachers during the 1980s. By combining a greater sensitivity to place with a more realistic explanation of the causes of patterns and processes, an acknowledgement of the importance of the political unit, and an involvement of attitudes towards issues, geography could be both enjoyable and important for young people.

Even if such a geography were desirable in theory, there are many constraints on its development in schools at the present time. Reference has already been made to cuts in resources for schools and for in-service education. Colleges of higher education have their own problems, and are unable to give the extensive support they provided in the early 1970s. Many teachers are also hard-pressed in their normal school activities, and are not always keen to get involved in yet more change. There is also every likelihood that with declining rolls and teacher redeployment more and more geography in lower schools will be taught by non-specialists at a time when there is pressure for accountability and getting back to basics in teaching—whatever that means. In practice it encourages a tendency to retreat to a formally defined and taught curriculum. These trends all combine to make the introduction of a humanistic geography of the sort described more difficult.

There are some encouraging signs. The Schools Council 16–19 Geography Project is based on a philosophy sympathetic to the humanistic movement. Although its immediate target is restricted to older students, its message is likely to affect many geography departments. The proposals for a common examination system at sixteen plus, with the identification of criteria that must be accepted by all boards, could be a powerful agent of change. The trouble is that much of the essential character of the humanistic approach is not readily amenable to assessment and examination. Nevertheless it is not unreasonable to expect some encouragement from those determining new trends, especially as the Schools Council geography committee and many leading members of the Geographical Association seem to be moving in this direction.

There is little doubt that good resource material is a positive agent for change, and it is likely that the 1980s will see the publication of textbooks and materials for geographers with this humanistic emphasis. Already there are examples in books such as *West Indies* (Wright, 1979), somewhat less explicitly in *Basic Geography* (Greasley *et al.*, 1979), *A Sense of Place* (Beddis, 1981) and the series *Geography and Change* (1982) published by Nelson. As with examinations, though, books alone may not be the main vehicle for a new approach. In the end it will depend on teachers who believe in it and have the energy and professionalism to translate these views into a geography programme.

One thing is certain: the wider world, the school system, and the teaching of geography will not stay the same for very long. Teachers have been saying for some time now that schools must educate pupils for a life of continual change. It is salutary to be reminded that we are a part of the world, and will ourselves be inevitably involved in these changes in an uncertain future. There is perhaps some consolation in the fact that while excessive change can be uncomfortable and exhausting, the years since 1960 have shown that, with a minimum of luck and a willingness to adapt, it can be both exhilarating and rewarding.

Further reading

P. Ambrose (ed.), *Analytical Human Geography* (Longman, 1969).
M. Chisholm, *Human Geography: Evolution or Revolution?* (Penguin, 1975).
Geography and Education, Ministry of Education Pamphlet No. 39 (1960).
D. Gregory, *Ideology, Science and Human Geography* (Hutchinson, 1978).
D. M. Smith, *Where the Grass is Greener* (Penguin, 1979).
Yi-Fu Tuan, *Topophilia* (Prentice-Hall, 1974).
R. Walford (ed.) *New Directions in Geography Teaching* (Longman, 1973).

Chapter 2

Reflections on the High School Geography Project

Nicholas Helburn

The High School Geography Project (HSGP) began to take form in the United States just twenty years before this writing. We've been through the confusion of what to do, the excitement of riding the crest of the wave, the discouragement when the product didn't sell very well, and a second chance with the publication of a revised edition.[1] This twenty years of American experience along with some contact I have had with the British Schools Council geography projects may give a useful perspective.

It was a confusing time at the beginning. No one person had a clear vision of where HSGP should go. William Pattison, the first director, brought together in conferences academic geographers, teachers, and educators, and from these contacts distilled a draft curriculum proposal. He got a dozen teachers released from their other classes so they could develop new materials. Nearby were academic geographers who agreed to serve as subject matter consultants. This model of curriculum development, with the teacher assisted by more expert help, is superficially like the British 14–18 and 16–19 Geography Projects. In the United States in 1962 and 1963 it helped individual geography teachers, but resulted in practically nothing which could be circulated to help more teachers.

Clyde Kohn brought together in a pamphlet the best he could gather from the work of those teachers, but it had little impact. Most influential was the incongruous Chapter 5 in which Edwin Thomas summarized his 'structure of geography', the theoretical statement of the new spatialism.[2]

It seemed to us who took over from Pattison in 1964 that the teacher-centred model of curriculum development would not work, that American teachers at least were not sufficiently well trained in the discipline to find its most powerful explanatory ideas. The prophets of the curriculum reform movement at that time were Jerome Bruner[3] and Joseph Schwab.[4] They asserted that we must 'have the courage to exclude' and develop materials which would help students understand and be able to use 'the structure(s) of the discipline'. There was a conventional wisdom within the Education Directorate of the National Science Foundation (roughly equivalent to the Schools Council in Britain) and amongst the academics who had been brought into the curriculum reform movement. This suggested that selection of the important ideas (concepts, structure) should be made by the élites of the discipline, who alone have the insight to distil the truly profound ideas. Then the work of developing the classroom materials which illustrate and teach these ideas can be developed by other academics and teachers.

HSGP shifted to a model of leadership consistent with this conventional wisdom. The steering committee was made up of geographers with university appointments and a strong allegiance to science. Gilbert White, then of the University of Chicago, was chairman of the steering committee and William Garrison, founding father of the quantitative revolution, was an influential member. I left my professorship at Montana State University to be the director. The first concern was that the material be 'good science'. Students should be learning powerful ideas and the content should reflect well on geography.

A part of our philosophy was that school administrators would have no objection to geography materials which were rigorous and challenging intellectually, that indeed they were seeking such if we could just produce them in a teachable form.

Our sister projects in biological and earth sciences were using writing conferences to generate materials. College and university scientists and secondary school teachers were brought together for a couple of months, divided into small teams, assigned part of an established outline, and given short deadlines to complete the prose. Editors and illustrators worked with the teams. Material was written, reviewed, edited, revised, rewritten in what seemed like a pressure cooker atmosphere. The result was a text which was thought to be good science, good prose, and well illustrated. The first version (in draft form) was used by teachers who were carefully selected. Their comments and criticisms were the basis for further editing and revision before going into final printing.

Reacting against the hectic and pressured atmosphere of the writing conference, HSGP chose to farm out the development of materials to small teams. Each team would be led by one or two university geographers working with teachers, other educational specialists and, where available, editors. They had enough time—six to nine months—and money to develop materials, have them tried in a few classrooms, and then revise them in the light of the classroom trials. Thus Arthur Getis of Rutgers University and his wife Judy, trained in geography and with teaching credentials, took the leadership of the first urban unit. Dana Kurfman, former teacher and then test developer for the Educational Testing Service functioned as their educational specialist. Five New Jersey teachers tried the initial materials. Similarly, Walter Killmorgan, then President of the Association of American Geographers, agreed to marshall the University of Kansas faculty to do the agriculture unit and Duane Knos gradually surfaced as the unit author. A review of these and other authors would corroborate the assertion that the initial orientation was toward positivist science.

This model of development allowed much greater flexibility than the writing conference. While the steering committee did finally reach virtual agreement on an outline, it was subject to revision. Indeed it was radically modified as the materials took shape. The writing conferences resulted in texts, but the unit authors were encouraged to think in terms of activities, structured learning situations lasting one or more class periods. Further, they were exhorted to invent different kinds of classroom procedures and a wonderful array of different activities came forth: ways of giving partial information so the student will seek more, ways of posing a problem so that a vigorous discussion ensues, ways of involving students actively in the learning process. Refinement, rewriting, selection and sometimes replacement, and editing in the HSGP office assured a coherent final product. But credit for the imagination, invention and variety should be ascribed mostly to the unit authors.

Looking back from 1981 on activities developed in 1965, it is easy to assert that they reflected the positivist attitudes of the time. We certainly felt we represented Science with a capital S.[5] One of the questions asked as we decided what to keep and what to throw out was: 'Did the students learn something? Something identifiable and meaningful?' We did not get the contrast between pre-test and post-test we expected, but we did get net gains in knowledge, understanding, and cognitive skills. Certainly we need not defend such materials as compared to the texts in common use with their over-load of factual information. But looking back we hear the questions: 'Were they good enough? Weren't they too strongly scientific? Did they develop only the left hemisphere, the rational side of the brain? Did they do enough with behaviour and with perception? Didn't they teach students to accept the status quo? Were not the values embedded in the HSGP materials such as to reinforce in students a respect for positivist science in a capitalist society?'[6] My answer to such questions (they are really charges rather than questions) must be 'yes' with qualifiers. To use a phrase not common on the American side of the Atlantic, 'I take your point, but . . .'

A few examples

i) The first activity in the *Geography of Cities*, the first unit of HSGP, draws on differential perception for the dissonance which drives the discussion. With very little introduction students are given a simple map, Figure 1, and asked: 'If you were a settler coming from Europe to North America, which site would you choose for a city?'

Studying the simple map, some of the class choose site A, some B, others C. The discussion which follows brings out most of the site and situation considerations, drawing out the previous knowledge and understanding of the class, reinforcing and widening the knowledge and understanding of individual students.

But there are at least two other educational objectives embedded in the activity. One is the overt recognition of assumptions. When the teacher asks 'Why didn't we all choose the same site?', it becomes clear that some considered hostile Indians to be a greater danger than pirates or European navies, while others assumed the Indians to have been pacified. Others assumed point A to be flood prone, or that D was at the fall line and therefore the natural break of bulk point at the head of navigation. The recognition of individual variation in the assumptions we bring to a task is not the subject matter of geography, but is important in communications and a fundamental of phenomenological philosophy.

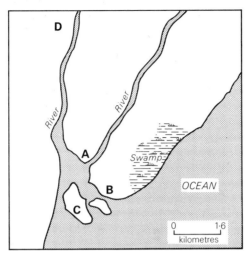

Fig. 1 *Four sites for a city in 1800*

The other embedded objective is the emotional sense of well-being which comes from using (and being recognized for using) previous knowledge in class. Too often the teacher assumes ignorance. It becomes habitual in the didactic, presentational mode for both teacher and student to assume the student must be told everything. In this first activity of unit 1 students get the positive satisfaction of contributing to the learning of the others from their own store of experience. This is a form of empowering. Repeated often enough it becomes liberating, provided of course that it is not cancelled by insults and sarcasm. And the extension of the activity into site selection west of the Appalachians ends with the conclusion that even after studying carefully the evidence, past and present, forecasts of the settlement pattern over thirty or forty years are likely to be very wide of the mark.

While positivist science recognizes the difficulty of forecasting, the frustration associated with failed forecasts is not a part of the usual indoctrination at secondary school level.

ii) Shock at how easily we can be misled is part of the emotional impact of the second activity in the *Geography of Cities*. Students are provided with stereoscopes and matched pairs of air photos of a portion of New Orleans. They study three adjacent neighbourhoods. The first includes both tiny older homes and what appears to be public housing, similar to council flats in Britain. The second contains larger homes with landscaped lawns and driveways. The third appears to be even newer with larger lawns and a park or golf-course nearby. The teacher asks the students to guess the socio-economic level and the racial composition of the three neighbourhoods.

Most American classes are easily drawn into the trap, guessing that the first neighbourhood is occupied primarily by poor blacks, that the second is intermediate, and the third is reserved for well-to-do whites. Then they are referred to the topographic map and a table of census data. Neighbourhood 1 is indeed occupied overwhelmingly by poor blacks, but neighbourhood 3 is occupied mostly by middle-class blacks, slightly less affluent than the whites in neighbourhood 2. Eagerly they go back to the air photos and the maps to discover what clues they might have used to avoid being misled. Neighbourhood 3, it turns out, is a part of the campus of Southern University, a dominantly black institution. Sceptics make better scientists, but scepticism is a value much wider than logical positivism.

iii) The Portsville activity was kept in the materials primarily for its emotional value. Here the students use tiny Lego-like blocks to build a city, modifying the site and taking into account changing functions and transport systems over five decades.

As we approached the final decisions on the manuscript, it was obvious that Portsville would keep the price of unit 1 considerably above traditional text materials. Was it worth the cost differential? The cognitive gain was not great enough to warrant the cost. What made us so reluctant to drop it? While we could not be sure, it was the consensus of the editing team that it was the emotional—perhaps spiritual—gain that made the activity crucial. Until one has played Portsville, one has never felt bigger than the city, one has never felt the power of being able to influence the direction of its growth. While we were self-conscious of the empowering value of the activity, we were not comfortable in sharing this publicly for we could ill-afford a public debate on the objectives in the affective domain.

At the time, in the 1960s, when we were asked about the objectives in the affective domain, we declined to answer the questions directly. We admitted that we were conscious of affect as a result of the activities. We identified the enjoyment of learning as an important goal. But among ourselves we felt that there was little agreement on goals in the affective domain among geographers or among teachers. We believed that a public debate about the emotional, spiritual, ethical, and political values developed or reinforced by the HSGP activities would have been destructive.

To some extent, the subsequent history of curriculum reform in the United States tends to corroborate our judgement. *Man: A Course of Study* (MACOS) appeared in final form soon after HSGP. Many of us had admired it as the best curriculum material in the social sciences. It used beautiful film episodes as the basis for middle school (ten and eleven year olds) student inquiry into the process of growing up, the elements of parenthood and the care of the young, and the functions of family. It required skilful teaching of a sort not widely practised in the United States, and was published with a required teacher-training component. When less enlightened parents realized the effectiveness of the material in liberating their children, they attacked the course. In Phoenix, Arizona, MACOS was put aside even though the majority of parents and teachers favoured it. In most American communities the school administration is so insecure that if a course is controversial they will avoid it regardless of how valuable it is. The MACOS controversy was so intense that it brought to an end the whole era of curriculum reform which started before Sputnik with the 'New Math' and included HSGP.[7]

iv) In our long, quiet, disorganized discussion with Duane Knos about his hopes for the material on agriculture for unit 2, he had some interest in the factual and conceptual gains by students. But in the game of farming, after making sure the children would be having a good time, his next concern was that they would empathize with the uncontrollable risks that farmers live with season after season. He achieves his goal. Students identify this as the most powerful result of playing the game. This is not indoctrination in the name of science. This is practice in seeing the world as others see it.

Knos seems to have succeeded in moving away from the traditional valuing of reasoned decision-making. A significant minority of teachers objected to the activity in spite of the fact that their pupils enjoyed it and learned from it. They found the activity offensive since it did not reward the 'good' student. They are accustomed to rewarding the student who studies the charts and calculates the data and searches the map for the right place. In the .game of farming the elements of chance are so great that the teacher cannot manipulate the outcomes to favour the industrious and accommodating student.

Another activity in the agriculture unit was based on five interviews, three with individual US farmers, one with a pair of Costa Rican farmers, and one with a group of Polish farmers and a Ministry of Agriculture official. The overt cognitive objectives include the similarities of concerns across regional, political, and ethnic contrasts: where will we find farm labour at a price we can afford? Must the government keep meddling in our affairs? How can we interest our children in taking over the farm and continuing our way of life? But the thing that brought a twinkle to Knos's eye and put emotion in his voice was the sense that students would find in the Polish interview classic personality types: the peasant—discouraged and fatalistic; the organization man—running the state farm according to the rules; the operator—succeeding on his own, often at others' expense; the manipulator—trying to keep control at any cost.

v) Howard Stafford and his associates in the Metfab activity deliberately built in ambiguity. There was no single correct solution (this was true in many of the HSGP activities). Further, most of the roles favour least-cost reasoning while the president's role looks to the future and leans toward a location which will capture the larger share of the market in the future.

In de-briefing the activity, students are asked: 'Why did your group choose Chicago for the new Metfab factory while these other two groups chose New Orleans?' Children will identify that the reason was that: 'Joseph played the president and Joseph always wins'. They will recognize personality and role as significant in the decision-making process.

Ripples in the pool

With the manuscript complete the editing team disbanded and this phase of curriculum development in geography ended, but the ripples from the HSGP splash spread in the normally placid pool that is geographical education.

There was some influence in Britain and in Canada, where Ontario particularly has an active programme. In the US most of the federal money went into teacher-training summer institutes. Some of us who had been a part of HSGP started the teacher training with great enthusiasm. Unfortunately, teachers who got the extra training often went into administration or supervision or on to higher degrees and out of secondary schools altogether. Others returned to their schools, but could not get the materials or were assigned to teach other courses. So even after a successful summer institute, there was only a handful of teachers using the materials the next year. The amount of money available was incongruously small compared to the enormity of the task. Most of us became discouraged and returned to our conventional academic careers.

Another ripple was felt in our own careers, for none of us approached our university teaching in quite the same way after the project as we did before. Each of the unit authors and their associates had been caused to think deeply about the learning-teaching process. A series of courses followed aimed at modifying undergraduate and graduate teaching. Our new colleagues in schools of education picked up the spirit of inquiry and incorporated it into their pre-service courses, but most new teachers reporting for duty for the first time still had as their model of teaching the same didactic, presentational, pour-the-information-into-their-heads model as was held by previous generations of teachers. Until we can modify university teaching in all disciplines so that lectures are but a small fraction of the undergraduate experience, we should expect this limited view of teaching to persist.

Without any sense of guilt, in the true spirit of self-criticism, it is appropriate that we ask the question, 'How could we have done better?' We could have been more explicit about research skills. Alan Backler, in his Global Studies in Geography Project at the University of Indiana, is building explicit instruction on research and writing skills into the student's text. We had assumed that those skills would be added by the teacher, but I suspect that Backler is right in providing the explicit instruction. The teacher can always tell the students to ignore the box at the bottom of the page that deals with topic sentences.

Some of us felt that the work of Robert Samples and associates would lead to more profound change. They had been a part of the Earth Sciences Curriculum Project. As they focused their attention on teacher training they were concerned about more openness in the classroom and the place of aesthetics and especially the encouragement of creativity. A subsequent set of their curriculum materials[8] consist of instructions to teachers on how to send children out of the classroom in groups to carry out challenging tasks, for example: to bring back evidence of change in the environment; to take a picture of power; to map something you cannot see (such as a sewer system); to identify a million of something (as blades of grass or grains of sand). In spite of our admiration, and our understanding that the kind of thinking children do with such assignments is quite different from what they do in traditional classrooms, the materials were not widely adopted.

If we had been more aware of the behavioural approaches, we could have included activities in which the children observe their own spatial behaviour, and that of others. Likewise it would be easy to add activities in perception and on cognitive maps. There were models of curriculum which made public policy issues the central focus and others which contained in every unit a regular succession of activities: an introduction, a central essay, a set of programmed instruction, and so on. Neither of these models seemed to fit our task. While both have been successful where used, neither has become so widely adopted as to be proven more successful.

The Biological Sciences Curriculum Project (BSCS) had enough resources to develop several different sets of material, targeted for different audiences. There were three different versions of the text with emphasis on different aspects of biology. A whole set of materials were developed for slow learners using participative laboratory activities. They were so success- ful that many teachers of regular students adopted them. HSGP had hoped to do the same but the idea was cancelled in its early stages. We started to develop a course based on a regional outline. Neither academic geographers nor the National Science Foundation were very enthusiastic about it and the programme was dropped, the same fate as our attempt to reach bright underachievers.[9] There is something of this targeting strategy apparent in the differences among the Schools Council projects in Britain with the 16–19 Geography Project and the Geography for the Young School Leaver Project aimed at different audiences.

As readers of this book look to the future, it may be worth giving some attention to the question of why curriculum reform efforts have been so unsuccessful. GYSL has had a wide adoption. It is too early to pass judge- ment on the 16–19 Geography Project, but the adoption rate for HSGP was disappointing in the US. Geography was not alone in this disappointment. An unusually thorough review of the response of the American school system to science (including social science) curriculum projects came to very pessimistic conclusions. In spite of major investments in science curriculum projects by the National Science Foundation from 1948 into the 1970s, the teaching of science in American schools remained much as it had been in the 1940s. It is not enough, apparently, to demonstrate that schools *can* do better in the intellectual development of children. Within the social system as a whole schools serve system maintenance as well as system improvement functions. In Western society preparation for boredom and frustration may be more important than preparation for thoughtfulness and creativity. No individual in the school system would admit to this. Each of us holds ideals of public education as a force for social betterment. The historical record, however, is ambiguous at best concerning schools contributing to the intel- lectual improvement of the general student body.[10]

The author and his wife, analysing the record recently, proposed that most teachers in most schools are so concerned with the socialization of students that they will not use inquiry materials. Discipline is more difficult in open classrooms. Obedience is easier to achieve with simple classroom procedures. Single right answers are preferable to multiple or ambiguous solutions when the teacher wants to reward the conforming student and penalize the others. Those who are not sure of their control of the classroom hesitate to turn students loose in group projects. Given the pressures of the teachers' workplace and the general expectations of their peers, it seems unrealistic to expect them to depart very far from traditional classroom presentation.

Well-meaning efforts toward the improvement of geography teaching should be cognizant of the powerful conservatism of school systems. There may well come a time when an imaginative and humane geography can flourish. In the United States it seems remote. William Carey, the executive officer of the Association for the Advancement of Science, sounds pessimistic. In an editorial in the journal *Science* he points to the declining federal investments in science education in spite of studies calling for 'a new commitment to excellence'. He goes on to state that 'If (federal), state and municipal governments . . . economize at the expense of science education in the schools, the road back to excellence will indeed be a long one.' [11]

In the last two decades in both the US and in Britain we have demonstrated that it is possible to develop exciting challenging materials for geography students. We know that we can train teachers to use those materials effectively. We know that there are schools that want to use them. But the evidence points to a conclusion that schools in general are not ready to adopt materials that make geography come alive in the classroom.

References

1 J. Stoltman, 'Round one for HSGP: a report on acceptance and diffusion', *The Professional Geographer*, 32, 2 (1980), pp. 209–15.
2 C. F. Kohn (ed.), *Selected Classroom Experiences: The High School Geography Project* (National Council for Geographic Education, 1964).
3 J. Bruner, *The Process of Education* (Random House, 1960).
4 J. Schwab, 'Structure of the disciplines: meanings and significances', in G. W. Ford and L. Pugno (eds.), *The Structure of Knowledge and the Curriculum* (Rand McNally, 1964).
5 W. D. Pattison, 'The producers: a social history', in D. I. Patton (ed.), *From Geographic Discipline to Inquiring Student*, Final Report of HSGP (Association of American Geographers, 1970).
6 J. Huckle, 'Classroom approaches: towards a critical summary', in E. Rawling (ed.), *Geography into the 1980s* (GA, 1980).
7 K. B. Wiley, *The NSF Science Education Controversy: Issues, Events, Decisions* (ERIC/CHESS and SSEC, 1976).
8 *Environmental Studies* (American Geological Institute, 1971).
9 N. Helburn, 'The development process, a personal view', in D. I. Patton, op. cit. (ref. 5), p. 38.
10 M. B. Katz, *Class, Bureaucracy and Schools: the Illusion of Educational Change in America* (Praeger, 1975).
11 W. D. Carey, 'Science education: rhetoric and reality', *Science*, 211 (23 January 1981), p. 339.

Section B   New perspectives

'The ultimate challenge, precious but costly, is to develop a truly personal type of knowledge, one that allows for emotion as well as thinking, passion as well as reason, and one that leads to an understanding of the self as well as to an understanding of the world.'
Anne Buttimer, 1978

'The basic argument of this structuralist approach is that the various subjects of the social sciences are not independent, nor even separate; one cannot be studied in isolation from the other. . . . At the core of social science and the study of society is political economy. Politics, economics, sociology, geography, psychology; all study aspects of behaviour constrained by the mode of production.'
Ron Johnston, 1978

'The fact that white kids are living in Essex or somewhere doesn't necessarily cut them off from black children living in South Africa, or Brazilian children living in São Paulo. The question is: how do we give our children the information about the lives of their brothers and sisters in other parts of the world, and how do we inspire them to empathize and to understand the economic forces which have created the conditions they live in?'
Chris Searle, 1981

' I believe that environmental education can only be justified at the present time if, through acquisition of knowledge *and practice*, it equips students to demand a greater role in the increasingly complex environmental decisions which future generations must take.'
Brian Goodey, 1980

Chapter 3

Behavioural geography

John Fien and Frances Slater

> 'The universe of geographical study may be divided into three
> realms: the nature of the environment; what we think about the
> environment; and how we behave in and alter that environment.'
> *Lowenthal*, 1967

How often is the word 'geography' preceded by an adjective? We read of
human, physical, regional, social, economic and urban geography; of historical, cultural and welfare geography. Lowenthal's classification of the
discipline's domain cuts through these traditional content divisions by
suggesting that it is concerned with three realms:[1]
i) the physical world of natural and man-made phenomena and patterns (the
first realm),
ii) human beliefs and values about the environment (the second realm),
iii) how people behave in and interact with the environment (the third
realm).

He thereby gives us a novel view of the conceptual unity that underpins
all branches of geography and which should lead us to emphasize the links
between the various realms in our teaching. Indeed, Lowenthal emphasizes
the interrelatedness of the three realms and maintains that each can be
completely understood and explained only within the context of the other
two. Opportunities for organizing learning experiences in all three realms
now exist and offer both the possibility and challenge to increase the
meaningfulness of geographical education.

For the most part, however, the attention of geographers and teachers has
been focused on the first realm of the *real world* or physical reality, whether in
regional contexts or in the analysis of spatial patterns and organization. Study
of the real world through objective observation, description, and explanation
has resulted in much productive research and brought rigour and analytical
strength to geography. The adoption of scientific method has yielded fruits,
but it has neglected the role of human perception and decision-making in its
explanation of the spatial patterns. Indeed, until quite recently, the discipline
of geography has lacked both the philosophical basis and the research
methods needed for the study of such abstract and subjective phenomena as
human thoughts, beliefs, and values concerning the environment. Where
geographers have ventured into such areas in the past or sought to relate them
to the first realm of physical reality their explanations often tended to be
naive and deterministic.

Behavioural approaches in geography were becoming strongly evident by
the late 1960s as a response to objective analytical geography. They offered
ideas and procedures for incorporating a study of the second and third

realms, those of environmental perception and behaviour, into the main-stream of geographical enquiry. Behavioural geography is founded on the belief that in daily life we all subordinate reality (the first realm) to the world we perceive and act in. In Lowenthal's words, 'we respond to and affect the environment, not directly, but through the medium of a personally apprehended milieu.'[2]

Since we all have our personal views of the world, an understanding of world patterning and order cannot be based upon assumptions of people making rational optimizing decisions based on complete knowledge of environmental relationships. Cities such as San Francisco and London would not have been built in earthquake zones or on flood-prone river terraces, nor would pastoralists underestimate the drought hazard of the American Great Plains or semi-arid Australia if such assumptions held.

Obviously the geography in people's minds does not conform to the realities of the physical world. Our filtered perceptions, cognitions, and beliefs about the environment are a powerful determinant of what we do in that environment. Consequently, a further behavioural dimension has been added to the physical, cultural, historical, and economic factors with which geographers have traditionally explained spatial patterns and environmental behaviour. Behavioural research has added new and subjective variables to geographical explanation—those comprising individual and group beliefs, values and responses about and to the environment.

Private geographies

While it is only in the last decade that behavioural geography has developed a significant body of research, it was as long ago as 1946 that J. K. Wright in a presidential address to the Association of American Geographers stressed the need for geographers to examine the implication of the idea that we act according to our beliefs about the environment and not in relation to more objective information. He urged geographers to consider: 'the geographical ideas, both true and false, of all manner of people—not only geographers, but farmers and fishermen, business executives and poets, novelists and painters, Bedouins and Hottentots—and for this reason it [geography] has to do in large degree with subjective conceptions.'[3]

Then, in a paper in 1961,[4] Lowenthal speculated upon the nature and origins of the environmental beliefs, preferences, and motivations that each of us has. He called each person's personalized collection of environmental knowledge and values his 'private geography'. While he stressed that each private geography is unique, he saw a shared perceptual experience based on our common capacity to perceive the physical realities of the earth through a variety of shared perceptual senses as the common foundation of all private geographies. For example, all of us, with the exception of the very young or those with particular mental or physical disabilities, are able to perceive and retain cognitive images of such things as the distinctive spatial arrangement of objects, the partition of space by individuals and groups, and the distinc-tive appearance and texture of buildings, land, air and water. However,

31

beyond the shared perceptual experience building a commonality into our world views, he believed that our 'separate personal worlds of experience, learning and imagination' have created individual mental geographies that diverge markedly among people in different cultures, from individuals within a social group, and for the same person at different stages of life.

Thus, private geographies are composed not only of those perceptions that are universal, but also some that are culturally conditioned and others that reflect personal idiosyncrasies. Private geographies may be said to comprise a *world view*, a *cultural view*, and a *personal view* of spatial and environmental relationships. Behavioural geography seeks to go beyond the shared world view to the more individual dimensions of private geographies in order to explain environmental decisions and behaviour and the spatial pattern they produce. It should also alert us, as geography teachers, to the fact that we have opportunities not only to educate that world view but to clarify and enrich personal views and examine their links with environmental behaviour.

The concept of perception

The major concept in behavioural geography is one that geographers have borrowed from psychology—that of *perception*. For behavioural geographers, perception is the key which unlocks the second and third realms of environmental beliefs, decisions, and behaviour. Techniques such as questionnaires, interview schedules, attitude scales, semantic differentials, and personal construct analysis are used to discover how the mind perceives and restructures the environment and how such perceptions, linked with knowledge of the first realm, are used to guide decision-making. Details of some of these techniques, all of which may be used in the geography classroom or in fieldwork, are provided later in this chapter.

For geographers, Yi-Fu Tuan[5] has defined perception as a two-stage process which includes: 'both the response of the senses to external stimuli and purposeful activity in which certain phenomena are clearly registered while others recede or are blocked out.' Thus, in the act of perception the mind receives spatio-environmental information and then transforms the messages into an image of the environment that satisfies one's immediate needs and accords with one's previous experiences and value system. Piaget used the term 'adaption' to describe this information filtering process.

Perception and cognition

Psychologists also define perception as a two-stage process, but for them both the reception and filtering of environmental information are performed by the senses *before* reaching the brain. Thus, for psychologists the filtering process is not one of adaption. It is a physical, not a cognitive, process in which the myriad sense data provided by the environment are reduced or otherwise transformed into a shape and volume capable of being absorbed by the human mind. The inability of the mind to absorb the details of multi-sensory images of the environment necessitates such pre-conceptual filtering.

Cognition is the term used by psychologists to describe the act of cognitive processing that geographers include as the second stage in their definition of perception. Thus psychologists would call the Great Plains farmers' ideas about drought cognitions rather than perceptions.

This may be only a semantic difference, but it is important that we are aware of it. For example, many researchers studying mental maps report that their subjects often leave out conspicuous landmarks when drawing sketch-maps of their neighbourhood or city. The question needs to be asked, however, whether these omissions are due to faulty perception in the psychological sense (the subjects have not seen the landmark) or due to partial cognition (the landmarks are only minor features in the subject's perception of the area). Bishop and Foulsham's[6] study of children's images of Harwich establishes very clearly that children do see their town differently from adults and that landmarks significant to them differ in scale from landmarks significant to adults. Architectural elements are less important than elements personally used or experienced—a finding well in accord with Piaget's concept of egocentricity.

Perception, cognition and behaviour

Downs and Stea[7] postulate that our environmental cognitions are stored in our minds as environmental images or cognitive maps. In everyday life cognitive or mental maps can be seen to serve the dual roles of (i) solving spatial problems and (ii) guiding environmental behaviour. In these two ways cognitive maps constitute the functional base for each person's private geography. They comprise personalized collections of environmental knowledge and values.

Spatial problems are those that require decisions about the locations of desired objects and places and the most efficient and pleasant routes for reaching them. Such problems occur at all scales from finding the way from one room to the next in a house, to trips to and from school or the supermarket, and extend as far as cross-country journeys, trips abroad and international migration movements. In this way spatial problems are an intrinsic, ever-present aspect of daily life. Our cognitive maps are the means by which they are solved. An exercise in cognitive or mental mapping is outlined later in this chapter.

The second function of perception and cognition is that of guiding environmental decisions and behaviour. The interaction between perception, cognition, and consequent spatial behaviour is controlled by our value systems as illustrated in Figure 2. The starting-point for any decision or act can be located in the real world which provides information that enters the mind via the senses. In the mind the perceptions are filtered through cultural and personal variables and one's value system to produce an environmental image. The mediating factor between the images in a private geography and eventual spatial behaviour is one's value system and the filters associated with it. The importance of values and such filters in the decision-making process has been illustrated in numerous studies, e.g. of the territorial behaviour of Protestants and Catholics in the Shankill Falls area of Belfast, the differing

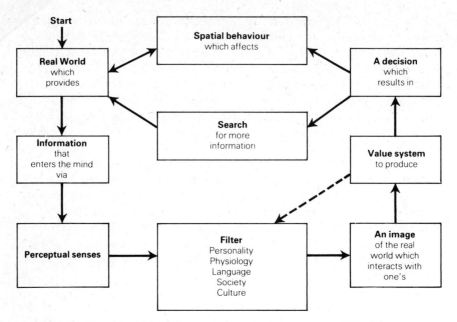

Fig. 2 A model of the relationship between perception, cognitive images, values, and behaviour

attitudes of hikers, canoeists, and speed-boat owners over the use of wilderness lakes in Canada, and the contrasting responses to natural hazards by subsistence pastoralists in Tanzania and commercial farmers in the United States. A brief elaboration of the latter example illustrates how variations in value systems affect decision-making and behaviour.

In the early 1970s a cross-cultural study of human adjustment to natural hazards was undertaken. A team, led by the geographer Robert Kates, used a standardized questionnaire to examine drought, flood, air pollution, and tropical cyclone hazard perception in a number of countries including Australia, Japan, USA, Tanzania, Bangladesh, Britain, and Hungary. One aspect of the study was centred on the relationship between the perceptions of drought and the range of management practices available to farmers in contrasting socio-economic and cultural regions. Figure 3 contrasts the possible adjustments to the hazard of drought suggested by American grain farmers and Tanzanian hoe cultivators.

In summarizing the contrasts, Saarinen[8] notes that the American farmers saw a more extensive range of possible adjustments to drought, 'including more related to farm practices and more requiring high-level technological input, such as construction of dams, ponds, terraces and irrigation. In contrast, the Tanzanians seem more flexible in terms of changing their life pattern. . . . While the Tanzanian farmer seems willing to move with an uncertain nature, his American counterpart seems willing to battle it out on a fixed site.'

While the educational and technological standards of the countries concerned have created socio-economic parameters within which the American

Tanzania			United States		
Adjustments	No.	Per cent	Adjustments	No.	Per cent
1 Move to seek land, work, food	51	36.0	1 Use dry land farming methods, mulching, summer fallow, etc.	78	40.0
2 Do nothing; wait	17	12.0			
3 Sell cattle, use stored food and money	16	11.5	2 Irrigation	46	24.0
			3 Alter landscape; dams, terraces, windbreaks, etc.	26	13.0
4 Rainmaking; prayer	15	11.0			
5 Irrigation	15	11.0	4 Use insurance savings, reduce expenditure	16	8.5
6 Change crops	9	7.5			
7 Change plot sites	4	3.0	5 No suggestions	16	8.5
8 Others	13	8.0	6 Others	12	6.0
Total suggestions	**140**	**100.0**	**Total suggestions**	**194**	**100.0**
Average suggestions/farmer = 1.07			Average suggestions/farmer = 2.02		

Fig. 3   *A comparison of suggested adjustments to the drought hazard in dry areas of Tanzania and the United States*

and Tanzanian farmers may operate, the particular mix of adjustments an individual farmer will select can only be predicted with reference to the individual private geography and perception of environmental relationships and values of the farmer concerned.

The application of perception studies to teaching

The role of perception in geographical studies is to help increase understanding of environmental decision-making and behaviour, activities in which we perceive, respond to, act on, and finally alter our surroundings. This requires teachers to deal with subjective elements of human responses to the world and acknowledge both the affective and cognitive domains of learning. Introducing students to the concept of perception, preferably through the exploration of their own perceptions, may well increase their sensitivity and lead to more considered environmental attitudes and behaviour.

Perception and fieldwork

One exercise which explored perceptions after a field study of the west coast of New Zealand achieved an increase in student understanding of knowledge and attitudes. A class of sixteen-year-old girls from the east coast of South Island studied aspects of the physical environment, settlement patterns, and economic activity of an economically declining area. After the trip the teacher tried to get the girls to organize their understanding around the following concepts which were related to resource use in the area: gold, sluices, coal, bush, aerial cableways, rimu, glaciers, Maoris, tourists, Europeans, and greenstone. The Maoris had come to the area for greenstone; the Europeans for gold, coal, and (latterly) timber (gold- and coal-mining leaving a legacy of sluices and aerial cableways in the landscape); and the tourists come for the scenic attractions offered by bush, glaciers, and mountains.

It soon became apparent that the girls were not happy with the list. To them the words were not at all representative of the dominant features of the west coast. In response to this, the teacher asked the girls to develop their own list of what were essentially their perceptions of the area visited. Their dominant responses included: glaciers, dredge tailings, rain, dirty rivers, rough pastures, bogs, lack of roads, lack of farms, hills, and bush. The girls were obviously most conscious of (i) what the area lacked *vis-à-vis* their own east coast environment which was prosperously farmed, though drought prone, with plenty of well-graded roads and high-quality pastures, and (ii) aspects of the natural environment which were most distinctly different, such as glaciers, bush, and the frequency of rainfall. By following up the exercise to incorporate the girls' responses in this way, they and the teacher learned a lot about their perceptions, levels of conceptual understanding, and attitudinal responses to the west coast environment.

To explore further these perceptions, the girls were asked to construct statements which they would use to test the way their parents and friends saw the west coast. The following three statements were voted to be the most appropriate:

1 I would like living on the west coast.   *Yes/No*
2 The west coast is an unspoiled part of New Zealand.   *Yes/No*
3 The west coast has a very bright future.   *Yes/No*

The girls considered negative replies to all three to be the 'correct' ones, though they expected greatest disagreement on the third—the government of the day was strongly and persuasively advocating the exploitation of an almost non-renewable resource, the slowly maturing, magnificent native forest, as one way of overcoming unemployment in the area.

The final exercise was based on viewing slides taken by the girls themselves as well as some from the geography teacher's collection. By a process of elimination, in response to the question 'Do you consider this slide to be typical of the west coast?', it became apparent that those slides which featured the brightly painted houses, small settlements strung out along the roads, or buildings of any kind were judged to be more typical than those featuring the high snow-capped mountains or bush-clad slopes. These large, well-known, physical features had been successfully supplemented by less spectacular details.

A possible extension of the exercise is one in which slides of the west coast are interspersed with slides from other parts of the country. Such an exercise might serve not only to build up a mismatch situation but to allow for an exploration of the similarities rather than differences between places and people. Equally fascinating work could be done in the local area by having students design questions and opinion statements about their home area in order to explore what their own town or locality means to them and other people. A semantic differential response form (Figure 4) could also be used for this purpose.

PERCEPTION OF URBAN AREAS

Instructions:

1   Here are pairs of opposing words with each pair separated by five spaces. On each line tick the space that best describes what you think about the area being studied. For example, if you think that 'man-made' features dominate, tick the space furthest to the left.

2   You may add extra pairs of opposing words if the perceptions you have are not listed.

1	man-made things dominate	natural things dominate
2	not much variety	much variety
3	ugly	beautiful
4	smelly	fresh
5	chaotic	orderly
6	poor	rich
7	boring	interesting
8	closed	open
9	horizontal lines dominate	vertical lines dominate
10	noisy	peaceful
11	old	modern
12	drab	bright
13	made for business	made for people
14	empty	full
15	hemmed-in views	distant views
16	impersonal	personal
17	threatening	friendly
18	sterile	exciting
19	unfamiliar	familiar
20		
21		
22		
23		

Fig. 4 An example of the use of the semantic differential in perception studies

Mental maps

Another way to explore the meaning of the environment for people is to ask them to list the first ten things they think of in relation to their town.[9] If information about their age, sex, length of residence in the area, and mode of travel to school or work is collected, the data can be classified and an attempt made to explain different perceptions of the town in relation to one or two of these variables. Alternatively Lynch's scheme[10] could be used to classify the list into landmarks, districts, nodes, paths, and edges. A frequency ranking of individual items in each category would provide for discussion. Why do so many of you list A, B, and C, and so on? Contrast environmental experience with environmental knowledge and ask your class to draw their collective mental map of their town. Are girls more restricted in their spatial range?

On a different scale the concept of neighbourhood may be explored by presenting students (or householders) with a street plan of the area in order to get them to delimit their neighbourhood. This can be done by asking them to mark all the places they visit regularly in the locality, the streets whose names they know, or streets where they know at least one person. A line can then be drawn around the 'known' neighbourhood. Analyse the size and shape of the neighbourhood. These attributes may be seen to vary with age, sex, length of residence, street patterns, mode and frequency of travel.

This line of investigation is closely allied to studies in action space. A possible action space exercise is to have students and their families record all the trips they make in a week. Maps of their action space may then be drawn. What is the general shape and direction of one's action space in a town or city? Why? Is there a difference between the students' action space and that of their parents or neighbours? In this, we are approaching the whole field of mental and preference mapping developed by Gould and White.[11]

Another approach to the exploration of mental maps is to ask students to draw from memory a sketch of their neighbourhood. With some teacher prompting we suggest that you ask students to put in as much detail as possible, including routeways, land uses, buildings, open space, landmarks, views, levels of activity, and their feelings about different parts of the neighbourhood. A day or two later allow students to check their perceptions by taking their maps and walking through the area. They should be asked to note how their maps differ from reality. What did they leave out? How did they alter what is there? What parts did they know best? Did they notice anything new as they walked through? They could then compare differences in their perceptions as highlighted by direct observation.

A simple mental mapping exercise which builds up a knowledge surface at a national level is 'How well do you know your country?' A map and a list of administrative units should be prepared and students asked to indicate how well they know them. For example:

Administrative unit	Very well	Moderately	Not at all well	Why do you know/ not know this area?
Avon		✓		My aunt lives in Bath and I visit her for holidays

Individual maps should be used to produce a choropleth map and points of similarity and difference discussed in class. The class should draw up a list of the reasons explaining the variations in the knowledge surface. The following are likely to be put forward: once lived there; visit friends there; visit relatives there; have played sport there; have been on a school trip there; have travelled through on way to . . .; have visited the . . . there; friends have told me about it; have read about it; . . . is there and it's often mentioned on TV.

The types of activities (visiting friends, playing sport) which promote high levels of knowledge could be identified and direct personal experience compared with indirect sources of information. Distance-decay principles and domes of desirability are probably operating and barriers may exist on a national scale—physical as well as cultural—to influence knowledge of a country. Major motorways and routeways may also influence knowledge and there may be special reasons to explain particular areas which are either very well known or not well known. A question to bring out the fundamental significance of the knowledge surface may go like this: 'If you were about to set up a new industry, where would you place it? Why?' A discussion of this question would reinforce the practical implications of perceptions and draw out the possible wider dimension of classroom exercises like this.

The repertory grid

The final technique for investigating people's perceptions of their environment to be suggested in this chapter is the repertory grid—a difficult technique to explain but simple enough to operate. It is based on personal construct theory which is used in psychoanalysis as a way of explaining people's behaviour in terms of the way the patient mentally constructs his/her world. First of all the patient would be asked to write down the names of people important in his/her life. The list might include mother, father, husband, wife, boss, son, friend. The therapist would then select three of these elements at a time and ask the patient in what ways any two were alike and how they contrasted with the third. The grid would be complete when all possible combinations had been made and the patient's responses recorded. The technique rests on the ability to make distinctions. For example, the mother and wife/husband may be seen as loving, the father as harsh. The persons named form the elements of the grid, the distinctions elicited begin to form the constructs. Diagrammatically, the repertory grid may be presented as in Figure 5. Gradually (for most people the matrix expands into twenty or thirty rows), the therapist comes to understand how the patient constructs his/her personal environment.

It is not difficult for a geographer or a town planner to see that this technique can be used to explore environmental perceptions and attitudes. One example must suffice. A group of Post-Graduate Certificate in Education students at the London Institute of Education had been using a section of Geography for the Young School Leaver programme to teach a class of difficult fourth-year girls and boys about new towns. A student, Elizabeth Allen, who had research experience with the repertory grid

Constructs	Elements				
	Mother	Father	Wife/husband	Friend	Boss
Loving/harsh	1	0	1		
Answers questions/tells you to find out for yourself	0	1			1
Holds the same values as myself/does not hold the same values			1	1	0
Believes success is the most important goal in life/does not believe success to be the most important goal		1		0	1
Is very like me in character/is not like me in character	1	0		1	
Generous/not generous	1	0	1		

Fig. 5 Sample repertory grid for personal construct analysis

technique, thought that it might be used in introducing the class to new town design. She simplified the exercise by pre-selecting the elements of the grid for the class; these are shown in Figure 6.

The first three elements (or triad) were named and an individual asked which she considered to be the most important and why. From churches, community centre, and factories, the latter was selected as the most important element because it provided jobs. There was general agreement with this

Constructs	Elements								
	Churches	Community centre	Factories	Health centre	Libraries	Shopping centres	Schools	Sports centre	Parks or open spaces
Needed for jobs			X						
Needed for food, clothes and furniture						X			
Needed for learning							X		
Needed for good health				X					
Needed for information									
Needed for leisure and relaxation									

Fig. 6 Part of a repertory grid for a new town study

reason. 'Needed for jobs' was recorded in the constructs column and a mark placed in the column headed 'factories'. The next triad—health centre, libraries, and shopping centres—was presented and a second member of the class chose shopping centres, the construct elicted being the fact that such centres are required for food, clothes, and furniture. In the third triad, schools were considered most important, the respondent affirming that there is a need to learn! Good health proved to be the priority when a choice among church, health, and libraries was requested. The elements were presented in triads until a dozen constructs had been drawn up. No attempt was made to present all possible combinations. The constructs were then used to dig more deeply into the functions performed by the elements. The class was asked to consider if other elements also provided jobs or were needed for food, clothes and furniture, for learning, or for good health. Further marks were placed in columns. Lively, constructive discussion and argument took place.

While therapists might not recognize this application of the repertory grid technique, the exercise proved to be a very useful way of (i) motivating a rather hostile class, (ii) eliciting students' perceptions of urban areas and services, (iii) evaluating these perceptions in relation to personal and community needs, and finally (iv) applying them in a town-planning exercise.

Education for self-awareness

The behavioural response to the dominance of the first realm in geographical studies is based upon a recognition of the concept of perception. The empirical investigations of behavioural geographers have demonstrated the actual integration of the three realms in many human-environment relationships and have provided realistic explanations of spatial behaviour. While these ideas should be introduced to students, we believe the real value of the behavioural response is to involve students in activities and enquiries where they will become increasingly aware of the perceptions and images that constitute their own private geographies. The value of this chapter depends upon its potential to encourage teachers to experiment with some of the ideas we have sketched out, to be motivated and interested enough to read further,[12] and to begin to develop and share perception-based exercises of their own.

References

1   D. Lowenthal, *Environmental Perception and Behaviour*, Department of Geography Research Paper No. 109 (University of Chicago, 1967).
2   D. Lowenthal, ibid.
3   J. K. Wright, 'Terra incognitae: the place of imagination in geography', *Annals*, AAG, 46 (1947), pp. 1–15.
4   D. Lowenthal, 'Geography, experience and imagination: towards a geographical epistemology', *Annals*, AAG, 60 (1961), pp. 241–60.

5   Yi-Fu Tuan, *Topophilia* (Prentice-Hall, 1974).
6   J. Bishop and J. Foulsham, *Children's Images of Harwich*, Environmental Education Research Report No. 3 (Kingston Polytechnic, 1973).
7   R. M. Downs and D. Stea (eds.), *Image and Environment: Cognitive Mapping in Spatial Behaviour* (Arnold, 1973).
8   T. F. Saarinen, *Environmental Planning: Perception and Behaviour* (Houghton Mifflin, 1976).
9   J. P. Stoltman, *Mental Maps: Resources for teaching and learning*, Teaching Geography Occasional Papers No. 32 (Geographical Association, 1980).
10 K. Lynch, *The Image of the City* (MIT Press, 1960).
11 P. Gould and R. White, *Mental Maps* (Penguin, 1974).
12 J. Gold, *An Introduction to Behavioural Geography* (OUP, 1980).

Chapter 4

Humanistic geography

John Fien

'A common suggestion which we make to our students is to find within themselves the geographer's "antennae" we are all born with. A person-centred approach seems to be an effective and functional way to enable personal exploration of spatial dimensions. Everything begins at the "awareness" level of Bloom's taxonomy of affective objectives rather than at the "content" level of cognitive objectives upon which most modern education is based.'
Romey and Elberty, 1980[1]

As with behavioural geography, humanistic geography's concern is with the areas of human-environment relationships that Lowenthal labelled the second and third realms of geography—our thoughts and feelings about the environment and the human-environment exchanges that result from them. Humanistic and behavioural geography share a concern to delve beneath the spatial patterns of the first realm—the real world out there as it exists in terms of cold objective facts—to the human motivations, perceptions, and values that create and modify landscapes and, in turn, are influenced by them. This renewed interest in the study of man as an important agent in physical and cultural landscapes has been one of the major developments in geography in the last decade. It parallels and, in part, complements the concern for social justice, relevance, and the quality of life expressed by welfare and radical geographers (see Chapters 6 and 7)—but at more personal, intimate levels.

The concept of man as a landscape agent was a neglected one during the quantitative revolution in geography because subjective concepts such as landscape values, perceptions, and actions were not readily responsive to study through the scientific, hypothetico-deductive mode of inquiry. However, the reassessment of purpose and methods in the discipline that occurred in the 1970s renewed and legitimized geography's concern with subjective concepts and the differences in human environmental behaviours, as well as the more generalized patterns that the scientific approach sought to emphasize. Nevertheless, while stemming from the same forces of change in the discipline's history, behavioural and humanistic geography have quite distinct philosophical perspectives, purposes, and research methods.

The humanistic tradition

Behavioural geography sees geography as one of the *social sciences*. It works, therefore, within the philosophical and methodological tradition of neo-positivism (science with a human face) and seeks to enhance the social, economic, and political explanation of geographical patterns by adding a consideration of the psychological factors that reflect differences in human perception and experience. Humanistic geography has advanced from the constraints imposed by scientific methods and aligns itself more with the *humanities*—those areas of study that explore the subjectivity of human responses to people, places, and events. Thus, like the historian or the novelist, the humanistic geographer seeks to provide people-orientated insights into the experiences, character, and purpose of human occupation of the earth.

From such a perspective, humanistic geographers define the subject as the study of the earth as the dwelling-place of man, emphasizing the experiential aspects of such dwelling. They define 'dwelling' in the existentialist sense of living closely to places (ranging in scale from one's home to the entire planet), feeling comfortable and at home in them, and taking responsibility for one's actions within them. This suggests a reorientation of geographical education towards helping students to become more aware of the experience of dwelling and its varied expressions in different times and places. Seamon[2] asks that students be given the opportunity to explore 'the simple and accepted aspects of daily life in relation to place and environment' so that they may recognize and enhance 'dwelling' in their own lives. This emphasis on dwelling leads humanistic geographers to see geography as a *process* rather than as a body of subject content. In the words of Romey and Elberty,[3] geography 'exists in the doing of it as much as in having the results of it'. Geography is something which is *lived*—as the reference to 'the geographer's "antennae" we are all born with' at the start of this chapter indicates. As Donaldson[4] explains: 'Every human being who perceives, explores, experiences, and acts in space is a geographer. . . . Being a geographer is nothing more than the necessary workings of the human mind.'

With a focus on the taken-for-granted geography of everyday life, humanistic geography seeks to amplify those aspects of human-environment relationships that are distinctly human, namely our perceptions, motivations, and experiences within the environment. This concern is indicated in the titles of books recently published by humanistic geographers—*Space and Place—The Perspective of Experience* (Tuan), *Children's Experiences of Place* (Hart), *Place and Placelessness* (Relph), *A Geography of the Lifeworld* (Seamon), and *Prisoners of Space: The Geographical Experiences of Older People* (Rowls). The authors of such books and numerous articles on similar topics are increasingly fulfilling the goals of the humanities *through* geography by providing insights into the character of human dwelling in a geographical world. In this way, humanistic geography is able to provide deeper understandings of the unique view of the world each of us has because of the subjectivity of individual experiences and values.

To use the terminology of Chapter 3, humanistic geography focuses on the *private geographies* from which academic geography is derived. Humanistic geographers thus remind us of the foundation of the discipline in the lived world of everyday life.

Private geographies

To a large extent our private geographies are an unconscious part of our actions and identities. They comprise the many memories, values, and skills that allow us to operate effectively in the environment. They assist us in making decisions about the location and attributes of the phenomena experienced in everyday life. Our private geographies thus have both *locational* and *evaluative* functions. The locational function is served by the images we hold of all the places we have inhabited, visited, imagined, and seen through the media. When a journey or landscape, for example, is too large for immediate perception, the cognitive image of it is recalled and used to plot a desired distinction relative to one's present location via all the known places en route. Rarely, however, is this an overt stimulus–response process as behavioural geographers claim.

Our private geographies are so much a part of our identities that finding one's way is often an automatic process. As one person recounted to Seamon,[5] who has made a study of everyday journey-making: 'You just get up and go; without thinking you know exactly where you have to go, and you get there but you don't think about getting there while you're on the way.' The concepts of 'body-habit' and 'place ballet' that Seamon has developed to explain the seemingly automatic nature of many of our daily geographical activities are an advance on the more mechanistic explanations of spatial behaviour provided by behavioural geography. Several of the activities suggested at the end of this chapter illustrate these concepts.

While spatial orientation and 'way-finding' are served by the locational elements of our private geographies, their evaluative dimensions have far wider applications. By providing guidelines for environmental judgements and decisions, they control what we do where, in, and to the environment. Consider, for example, the differences between environmental beliefs and activities of local residents and tourists in an area. Several studies have been undertaken to explore such differences.[6] In one case, Lerup[7] investigated the beliefs and activities of the local fishing people and those of holiday-makers in several villages in western Sweden. A review of his study illustrates the influence of the evaluative dimension of private geographies in everyday life and in the formation of landscape patterns.

For the local fishing families the sea is both a source of wealth and, from past experience and folklore, a cause of death. Thus they have mixed feelings of fear, gratitude, and respect for the sea. The spatial arrangement of the village reflects this. Along the wharves are many storage sheds for salting and storing the hoped-for catches. The houses, however, do not cluster around them or the water's edge. Instead, they are widely spaced and strung out up the coastal hillside to provide each house with an unobstructed view of the sea. A rich folklore of songs and stories has developed depicting the wives and children of the fishermen waiting, longingly, at the windows for the fishing boats to come in. The whole settlement is a manifestation of the relationship between man and the sea. However, the fishermen rarely think of going for a swim, indeed most of them do not even know how. As Lerup says, for them 'the sea is life and death, inexorably intertwined beyond man's comprehension.'

In summer the fishing families move to the basements of their homes and rent the top two floors to holiday-makers from the city. These upper floors, with their open vistas, provide the visitors with opportunities to gaze out of the windows and speak in admiration of the beauty of the sea, the colour and shape of the clouds, and the quaint fishing-boats moored at their piers. The holiday-maker spends his days swimming and sunbathing on the rocks and jetty in front of the storage sheds. For him the sea, the sun, and the village are no more than instrumental necessities for an enjoyable holiday.

Lerup's study reminds me of so many places I have visited, where I have been little more than an interested outsider watching life go on around me—the Moroccan oasis village, the Greek market, St. Peter's Square on Easter Sunday, the Welsh village pub. As an Australian brought up to love wilderness areas, I can remember being bored walking on the South Downs with English friends who were captivated by the landscape. In this respect their private geographies had little in common with mine. And even among the insiders of such environments, many contrasting human-environment interactions are provoked. This is because the particular environmental evaluations and sense of place that each person takes from a landscape are unique, reflecting individual experiences in the place, personal history, age and sex differences, and even one's imagination and mood at the time. For as Meinig[8] noted, even if we can try to look in the same direction at the same time, it is still not possible for us to see the same thing for 'any landscape is composed not only of what lies before our eyes but what lies inside our heads'.

Education for environmental competence

In seeking to amplify 'what lies inside our heads' in relation to everyday environmental activities and values, humanistic geography has important educational implications and advantages. In a period when educational basics are strongly emphasized, humanistic geography provides guidelines to what should be geography's basic educational purpose—the development of environmental competence. With its emphasis on lived experience, humanistic geography can be used to make students more conscious of their geographical ideas and actions, and better able to use the environmental knowledge and skills of their private geographies in the way-finding and environmental decision-making tasks of everyday life. While developing a heightened consciousness of their own private geographies, students may also become more aware of those of others, and so increase their level of empathy for the environmental beliefs, situations, and experiences of people in similar and different parts of the world. This is, I know, a liberal interpretation of the back-to-basics philosophy. However, it does highlight a necessary *raison d'être* for geography's inclusion in curricula whose goals are directed to the preparation of students for the experiences of adult life.

Geography teachers cannot do this by providing students with knowledge about academic geography. There needs to be a return to the basic everyday environmental experiences from which academic geography is derived. It is to the lifeworld of private geographies that we need to direct our attention if geographical education is to help students relate successfully to their own environment, play a role in its future development, and increase their level of empathy for other people's experiences.

There are important epistemological differences between the types of knowledge found in private geographies and those of academic or school geography.[9] These differences chiefly lie in the systematic and disciplined nature of the latter. Where private geographies comprise personal and cultural views of the world and are coloured by intimate and individual environmental meanings, academic geography provides a methodically derived, largely objective and generalized view of the world. It emphasizes the shared public meanings we need to understand in order to carry out many of our basic environmental transactions. Both types of geographical knowledge have their place in geography teaching as neither can be fully understood without the other. Our students' private geographies need to be refined, extended and enriched through contact with the concepts and methods of academic geography. We need to utilize the latter's subject matter and skills to help students discover order and meaning in their private geographies. On the other hand, academic geography is nonsensical as an educational medium without reference to the routine everyday environmental experiences and private geographies from which it was derived. However, a consideration of our students' private geographies and their environmental needs and interests, *not* syllabus guidelines to course objectives and content, should be the starting-point in all our course planning. As John Dewey observed, 'It is not a question of how to teach the child geography, but first of all, the question of what geography is for the child.' This humanistic perspective stresses that curriculum development in geography should be focused upon the private geographies of students and should aim to help students understand the knowledge, values, and skills contained in them in more systematic, effective and fruitful ways.

A learner-centred approach

One of the major failings of geography teaching to date has been the disproportionate attention we have paid to formal geographical knowledge. In so doing, we have largely ignored the experiential foundations of the discipline in the everyday geographical experiences that comprise the private geographies of our students. We have been too subject-centred in our teaching, acting as if geographical knowledge lies outside our students' experience and that they are merely the receivers of the subject matter we present. Such assumptions about learners and education ignore the fact that all people are meaning-makers, not only of environmental experience but also of school knowledge. Irrespective of what we teach or how we teach it, students will make a meaning of it that is all their own. They will relate the idea or skill to their own experiences and incorporate it into their own individual scheme of things. Thus each student creates a world of his or her own, and what becomes important in it is the meanings he or she had made of what we teach, not our intended meanings.[10]

In failing to take account of the meaning-making activities of students and of the active geographical lives in which they are daily engaged, we have ignored the very essence of the discipline and, unfortunately, that part of it that has most bearing on our students' lives. Only rarely can teaching programmes that are guilty of this provide meaningful educational experiences. For the most part they tend to do little more than stick on the frills of education. In so doing, we are in danger of creating a gulf between a student's private geography and his school geography with the latter being perceived as an intellectual pursuit that has little bearing on the spatial problems of everyday life and, consequently, of little import in the process of education for living. The problem put bluntly is this: examination boards, syllabus developers and, alas, too many teachers have too often seen geography as a ready-made body of knowledge to be acquired. Unfortunately, this view of geographical education and the teaching and evaluation procedures it implies can do little to activate or amplify the meaning-making environmental experiences in the everyday lives of our students.

Such learner-centredness requires a change in syllabus and classroom philosophy and practice. The learner-centred approach to geographical education accepts the active private geographies of students as the starting-point in curriculum planning. It seeks to enhance and refine students' understanding of the world through a study of people's (including their own) relations with natural and cultural landscapes, their environmental beliefs, and their responses to experiences of different environments. This humanistic approach to geographical education asks students to reflect upon geographical activities with the ultimate purpose of achieving a better understanding of man and his human condition. In order to educate a person geographically, we need to attend to that person's private geography, to the particular environmental images, beliefs and attitudes, spatial skills, and ways of organizing environmental knowledge that he already possesses. Such attention will reveal where inadequacies occur, where concepts need clarifying and detail added, and where contact with specialist geographical knowledge and procedures would be educationally beneficial. In this it constitutes a form of learner-centred education, but one within the controls of a discipline's conceptual and methodological framework. Through the interaction of the two forms of geography, the student's ordinary everyday ways of dealing with environmental experiences can be improved and his private geography made more disciplined and systematic and a conscious rather than unconscious dimension of his mind.

How is such an approach to geography teaching to be implemented in schools? In the short term it will probably not be possible with classes studying for externally controlled examinations. However, it is feasible with middle and lower secondary school pupils and maybe CSE Mode 3 classes. Successful experiences with the humanistic approach to geographical education with students in such classes may create a grass-roots movement for change in examination syllabuses. That learner-centred approaches in geography are manageable at such levels and even higher is well proven in the work of Romey and Elberty in New York. They have been conducting such courses most successfully since 1971.[11] The British educational system is far more rigid than the American one, however. Consequently, in the short term, changes from content-dominated courses to learner-centred ones will have to occur in middle and lower secondary schools first. To this end the educational implications and teaching ideas suggested in the rest of this chapter are directed to these levels of education.

Confluent education

The approach to teaching that I am recommending for such classes has sometimes been referred to as *confluent education*.[12] Confluent education emphasizes the bringing together of experience and knowledge—of affect and cognition—and in geographical education, of private geographies and academic geography. It has as its goal the education of a *feeling-thinking* person, not one in whom either aspect of the mind is ignored. Confluent education when applied to the tenets of humanistic geography has many implications for the content of courses, teachers' roles, and classroom atmosphere.

Course content

Course content, as I indicated earlier, will need to become learner-centred. This does not mean that students will only study what interests them, as some critics of learner-centred teaching suggest. Instead, by starting with the

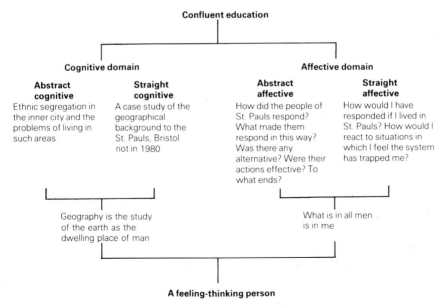

Fig. 7   Confluent education applied to a geographical example

environmental experiences of students and helping them to clarify their environmental values and self-knowledge, we can then ask students to consider the cognitive and values aspects of environmental issues and problems.

Let us take as an example the race riots in St. Pauls, Bristol, in early 1980. Figure 7 reveals how this issue may be studied from the perspective of confluent education. Note the learner-centredness on the affective side of the diagram and the way students are asked to clarify their own position, and apply it to a real (cognitive) issue with the ultimate goal of producing a feeling-thinking person.

In terms of overall course content Figure 8 contains the broad outline of a course structured around the private geographies of students.[13] This course seeks to relate students' environmental experiences to those of other people and to the environmental decision-making processes in society. No content detail, case studies, depth of study or class level are specified, however, as such considerations can only be determined by teachers once they know their classes. However, later in the chapter several teaching ideas that could be used in such a course are suggested.

Such courses would, I believe, meet the goals of humanistic geography and confluent education. They would probably be problem- or issue-orientated and transdisciplinary in scope, providing for a more holistic coverage of human-environment relationships than do many existing geography or integrated humanities courses.

COURSE THEMES

1 An examination of basic human needs such as clothing, food and shelter, and students' feelings about food as it is eaten, clothing as it is worn, homes as they are inhabited and wider environments as they are experienced.

2 An examination of secondary needs such as places of work and recreation and places as a source of identity and emotional security.

3 A consideration of human needs as sources of creativity such as housing design and interior layout, neighbourhood planning and landscape architecture.

4 A consideration of how man is related to the environment—the source that fulfils his needs—and the interrelationships between man and nature.

5 An examination of 'good' and 'bad' in the environment and the values that underlie such perceptions.

6 An examination of the factors underlying students' and other people's attitudes to the environment—probing the question of human values and the priorities we have set for our and other people's existence.

7 A consideration of levels of caring for the environment and other people and the nature of environmental behaviour appropriate to the values of each student.

8 An exploration of how change is effected in people's environmental preferences and behaviour.

9 An examination of the environmental decision-making and planning processes in society and of how change occurs in the environment.

10 A consideration of the role the individual can play in such change.

Fig. 8   A broad outline for a course based upon the private geographies of students

Teachers' roles

Confluent education demands that teachers serve as facilitators of learning, gradually dropping their traditional directive roles. Basing their suggestions upon the educational ideas of Carl Rogers,[14] Romey and Elberty[15] list three personal qualities that teachers would need to develop—an unconditional positive regard for all students, congruence (the ability to be genuine and honest about personal feelings during transactions with students), and empathy (the ability to sense the private meanings of students as if they were one's own). Such skills and the emphasis upon private geography over academic geography do not preclude the need for teachers to be thoroughly steeped in the skills, knowledge, and mode of thought of the discipline. Indeed, with the need to be continually responsive to learners' needs and interests, detailed lesson preparation would be difficult. Consequently, with the direction of lessons controlled by teacher response to student needs and suggestions, the major resources the teacher can offer are himself and his training in geography with its particular set of concepts for structuring environmental experience and its disciplined approach to inquiry and reflection.

Classroom atmosphere

The emphasis on teacher-student interaction as the guide to course development and the personal nature of many areas that can be explored in courses based upon humanistic geography and confluent education emphasize the need for a warm supportive classroom atmosphere. An atmosphere of mutual trust, respect, and risk-taking does not simply happen as a result of teacher and students being together over a period of time. Teachers are instrumental in creating such an atmosphere by their attitudes and actions from their very first meetings with a class.

Such a classroom atmosphere would enable students to feel safe and confident to express their own feelings and perceptions about the environment and their place within it. Learner-centred courses in geography demand open-ended learning experiences so that students can explore, clarify, and make their own meaning of the resources and ideas presented to them. Textbooks such as *Where You're At* and *Utopia* (both Penguin Education), *A Place to Live* and *Pencils in the Sky* (both Harrap), and *People in Places* (Prentice-Hall) contain many examples of appropriate open-ended exercises. I would think that all are very suitable for use with students in the first three years of secondary school. Similar experiential exercises and teachers' comments on their success and problems in using them are to be found in the *Bulletin of Environmental Education* and in the reports and forthcoming publications of the Schools Council Art and the Built Environment Project. I have found exercises based upon landscape appreciation, townscape notation, streetscape, sensory walking, and building appraisal from such sources to be successful and enjoyable learning experiences.

Some classroom activities

The following activities are designed for possible use in a course based upon the outline provided in Figure 8 and are examples of the application of humanistic geography and confluent education to geography teaching. The activities come from the various publications mentioned in the preceding paragraph, especially *People in Places*,[16] and my own work with students. The activities are expressed as general open-ended instructions to students with a view to teachers evaluating the possibilities of each for their classes and finding their own ways of introducing, expanding, and incorporating them into their courses. I have based the activities upon six aspects of humanistic geography that I believe to be relevant to middle and lower secondary school pupils—place memory, sensing the environment, place meaning and feelings, spatial range, feelings of environmental constraint, and resolving environmental conflicts.

A Place memory

1   What is the first place you remember? Describe it in as much detail as possible. What specific events can you recall happening there? What makes this place so memorable? What do some of your classmates think of your ideas?

2   Where do you remember having the most fun and/or the saddest experience of your life? Did the physical features or the mood of this place have anything to do with your feelings? If so, try to describe the place in detail and how it affected you.

B Sensing the environment

3   Go to a place in the school environment where you feel comfortable. Sit quietly there, concentrating on your senses and feelings. Spend 3–5 minutes on each sense in turn—seeing, touching, smelling, listening, and, maybe, tasting. Make lists of key words or phrases to record your reactions from each sense. Use your list (perhaps in comparison with other students' lists) to see what senses produced similar and/or different feelings. What senses dominated? Why?

4   Reproduce your overall impression of the place for another person. Appeal to as many senses as possible—try using a series of photographs, a poem, a drawing, a tape recording and/or a collection of things to feel and smell.

5   Go to a place many people visit for weekend outings. Why do they go there? Do you enjoy going there? How picturesque is it? What sort of things do people do there? Make a set of drawings or photographs to show why people like to go there.

6   Pretend you are the place in activity 5. How does the place feel having you and other people in it. How might it want people to alter their actions there? Would these changes be for the good?

C Place meaning and feelings

7   Do you like where you live? Why? What is it like to live in a house or neighbourhood you don't like? If you couldn't live in the house you have now, what sort of place would you like? Why? Why do you rule out other

types of residences? If you had to change neighbourhoods or even towns, where would you go? Why?

8   Make a collection of photographs or pictures of scenes you like. Write 50 words on each one explaining your reasons. Show your collection to some of your classmates. In turn study their collection. Do you have any scenes in common? What makes for this shared experience? Try to convince members of the group who disagree with your choices to change their minds. Is this easy to do? Why? Was it right to have tried to do it?

9   Repeat activity 8 for a series of scenes or places you do not like.

10   Interview people you find in places you like/dislike. Are their reactions the same as yours? Why?

11   Are there places you can visit when you feel depressed? Does being there help? Where do other people go? Ask several people this question and compare different types of places and people and the reasons they give.

12   What makes school grounds good school grounds? What could you do to transform your school into the sort of place you could really like? Shopping centres, parks, houses, and even towns could be used instead of school grounds for this activity.

D   *Spatial range*
This concept, along with those of activity space, cognitive distance and mental mapping, is drawn from behavioural geography. The activities suggested here indicate ways of applying the learner-centred principles of confluent education to them.

13   Identify the places you can visit within a 30-minute walk of your home. Produce a time-distance map of these places with home at the centre. How would the map differ if you were a blind or elderly person? Produce maps of places you can visit within 30 minutes of your home if you cycle or use public transport. How do all your maps differ? Which of your maps would be closest to those of a blind or elderly person? Why?

14   Identify some routes you use regularly. Why have you made these a part of your geographical activities—habit, speed, convenience, interest, beauty? For one week try travelling a slower route than one you especially use for speed. How did it affect your plans, habits, and feelings? Try using an alternative route to one you use for its scenic qualities. Deliberately try to find scenic things on this route. How does the new route affect your perception of the old one? The new one? Are there any journeys you make semi-automatically without having to think of them? What routes are they? Do they have anything in common to make them so habitual?

E   *Feelings of environmental constraint*
15   Are there any places in your school, neighbourhood, or town in which you do not feel free to move as you wish? Where are they? Why do you feel constrained in them? Do other people feel the same way? What changes are needed to make these 'safe' places?

16   Choose a place (bus stop, school office, car park, park, etc.) and make a list of the written and unwritten rules that apply to its use. Are there different rules for different places? Who makes the written rules? How are they communicated and enforced? Why? Spend 30 minutes in your chosen place watching to see if people obey the rules. What makes them obey the rules? What happens when they do not?

17   Visit the central part of your town with an old person, a child, a blind person, or a newcomer to the area. Keep to their pace and go exactly where they want to go. Try to keep the person talking about his or her feelings about the environment and how it affects them. How is the town centre supportive, inconvenient or hazardous for them? What do they think of other parts of the town in these regards? Do you share their feelings of enjoyment, annoyance and/or danger in various parts of the town?

F   Resolving environmental conflicts
18   Identify a conflict in the use of space in your area. Investigate all aspects and opinions about the conflict. What do you feel about it? How do the various opinions and suggested solutions affect you? Develop your own ideas for resolving the conflict. How would different people in the community react to your suggestions? What are the civic regulations in your area for resolving environmental conflicts? Who made them? What part do they allow individual people to play? Do people take advantage of the opportunities provided? Why or why not?

These eighteen activities are offered as ideas for teachers to develop into whole courses or sections of courses, matched to the learning objectives that best suit the students involved. They are on limited aspects of humanistic geography and mainly deal with the urban environment. This reflects the limited length of the chapter and the home environment of most of our students. However, equally exciting work can be done on the perception, use, and modification of natural landscapes and in the area of environmental ethics. For example, how and why do students and other people react to the energy crisis, wildlife extinction, wilderness, litter, and heritage environments? I believe the consideration of such issues and the activities I have described meet the goals of humanistic geography through the use of confluent education strategies and, thus, help students to probe, clarify, refine, and extend various aspects of their private geographies. If geographical education is to achieve its basic goal of environmental competence for all students, it must start with their private geographies and seek to raise their levels of self- and environmental-consciousness. In this way, the limits on personal freedom of meaning-making and the range of options for environmental activities and change imposed by subject-centred approaches to geographical education can be lifted. Students can thus be provided with opportunities to raise their level of environmental awareness to incorporate the more academic considerations necessary to formulate and implement places for acting in the environment and changing it in ways that suit them and their fellows.

References

1 W. Romey and W. Elberty, 'A person-centred approach to geography', *Journal of Geography in Higher Education*, 4, 1 (1980), pp. 61–71.

2 D. Seamon, 'Phenomenology, geography and geographical education', *Journal of Geography in Higher Eduction*, 3, 2 (1979), pp. 42–50.

3 W. Romey and W. Elberty, op. cit. (ref. 1).

4 O. F. Donaldson, *Children are Geographers: Explorations in Space*, National Council for Geographic Education Instructional Activity Series, No. 1A/E-12 (1975).

5 D. Seamon, *A Geography of the Lifeworld* (Croom Helm, 1979).

6 Yi-Fu Tuan, *Topophilia: A Study of Environmental Perception, Attitudes and Values* (Prentice-Hall, 1974).

7 L. Lerup, 'Riddles and unriddling', *Ekistics*, 234 (1975), pp. 300–5.

8 D. W. Meinig, 'The beholding eye: ten versions of the same scene', *Landscape Architecture*, January (1976), pp. 47–54.

9 J. F. Fien, 'Towards a humanistic perspective in geographical education', *Geographical Education*, 3, 3 (1979), pp. 407–22.

10 N. Postman and C. Weingartner, *Teaching as a Subversive Activity* (Penguin, 1969).

11 W. Romey and W. Elberty, op. cit. (ref. 1).

12 G. I. Brown, *Human Teaching for Human Learning: an Introduction to Confluent Education* (Viking Press, 1971).

13 J. F. Fien, 'Operationalizing the humanistic perspective in geographical education', *Geographical Education*, 3, 4 (1980), pp. 507–32.

14 C. Rogers, *Freedom to Learn* (Charles E. Merrill, 1969)

15 W. Romey and W. Elberty, op. cit. (ref. 1).

Chapter 5

Geography through art

Eric Brough

> 'I am against the terms "fantasy" and "symbolism" in themselves.
> All our interior world is reality—and that perhaps more so than our
> apparent world. To call everything that appeared illogical fantasy,
> fairy tale or chimera would be practically to admit not understanding
> nature.' *Marc Chagall*

So many people worry or complain about schools. If schools did a better job, they say, society would have fewer problems. As a teacher, I can only agree. We begin to differ when we attempt to define 'a better job'. How many adults (even ourselves as teachers) really believe that school taught them much that proved relevant in adult life? For most people, the only relevant part was their training in the three Rs, or in particular job skills.

Yet most of us remember with pleasure one particular teacher or even (amazing after all these years!) one particular lesson when time flew and the bell left us thirsting for more. We may know members of an older generation whose love of good literature or music was engendered in an elementary school classroom—a room devoid of all the expensive trimmings now considered essential, a room filled with pupils destined to leave school at thirteen for a lifetime of manual work.

I am not for one moment suggesting that schools in the past were all doing a better job. What had taken place in the classroom of the anecdotes and, of course, still happens on cherished but, alas, rare occasions, was true education—a meeting of minds.

Instrumental schooling

I think it is important to point out here that I find it difficult to talk about geography teaching as distinct from simply 'teaching'. Of course, with the ways schools are organized today, and probably for a very long time to come, we are faced with a separation of subjects and we have to select and organize our curriculum along these lines. Nevertheless, I believe that the true principles of education, which acknowledge no subject boundaries, must be always at the forefront of our minds. The curriculum is a mere tool and its success will depend almost entirely on the skill of the teacher.

In 1971 Bruner wrote, 'If I had my choice now, in terms of a curriculum project for the seventies, it would be to find a means whereby we could bring society back to its sense of values and priorities in life.' Isn't this what committed teachers, including geographers, should be trying to do?

It is unfortunately true that much of what has happened in schools past and present was not merely poor education, it was anti-education. A brief look at education in the past shows how easily it becomes instrumentalized. The monastic schools ignored vast areas of human knowledge and experience, and later the state schools of the nineteenth century trained children by rote in the three Rs, that type of training being all that was considered necessary for the kind of work the children would eventually do.

We pride ourselves on a greater sophistication, but are we being honest with ourselves? Is it not that many teachers judge their performance by those students who leave equipped for the specific jobs of the technological age and manage to overlook others, whose future role in society is less easily defined, and who leave feeling that time and energy have been wasted?

Perhaps vocational training *is* part of a school's purpose, but let us not delude ourselves that in providing it we are behaving differently from the arithmetic teacher preparing his pupils for the counting-houses of the last century. It is, more than ever, the burden of the teacher not to confuse 'the raiment with the man'.

Towards a wider view of man

It is tempting for geographers to study man as a social and physical being, observing him as the naturalist observes an animal—producing a study of habitat and habits. This approach is too limited because it ignores the feature which distinguishes man from other animals—his heightened spiritual awareness. To contemplate this dimension of humanity is to enter the realm of intangibles and uncertainties which leads to questions of ethics, philosophy, and religion.

Man, it seems, is the one creature with the sure and certain knowledge of his own mortality. Aware of the transience of everything he touches, he might be excused for putting minimal efforts into the fashioning of this world. Yet the opposite seems to be the case. The need for shelter becomes the frozen music of architecture, the urge to communicate becomes inspired poetry. All through the ages, timeless and universal, aesthetic and creative urges have pervaded every aspect of human life. These set man apart, and ensure that his greatest achievements speak across centuries and continents, constantly and consistently.

Ambivalent man journeys to the moon like a god, but stands on a deserted seashore like an ant. Man, whose hand may be shattered by one blow, may with one finger destroy the whole planet. A sometimes hopeless victim of his own frailty and mortality, he is nevertheless exhilarated and elevated by his power to create and change. Michelangelo produced David; Shakespeare, Hamlet.

The role of the teacher

In their early years children develop an awareness of self as distinct from the rest of the world, and at the same time perceive the relationships between themselves and the rest of the world, animate and inanimate. The perception of these relationships enables reconciliation of the individual with the community and the environment, and assists in the making of value judgements. This is an essential and major part of the development of the human being. We perceive through our senses and the education of these senses might be called aesthetic education.

The development of aesthetic awareness is, of course, a natural process, and it would take place in a society without schools. On the other hand, any aspect of development may be improved or refined, and students throughout the ages have sat at the feet of their masters, recognizing the extent to which their own talents and appreciation might be enhanced. There is an urge in all people to extend and develop those perceptive powers on which aesthetic awareness is built. To stifle this urge (even by ignoring it) is to deprive a person of the basic substance of his nature. His spirit, like the body deprived of its vitamins, is diminished. His humanity is denied.

Teachers must preserve and intensify the vividness of sensory experience and help pupils relate action to feeling, and reality to ideals. Idealism would then become not an escape from reality but a background criterion determining a response to it. Education's task is to help children to develop aesthetic sensitivity which will enable them to evaluate their experiences and make intelligent choices and judgements, a task more pressing than ever in the present world.

The appreciation of beauty

The artists of ancient Greece formulated a concept of beauty based on mathematical proportion. Centuries later, scientists lifted their eyes from the microscope and pronounced that these same mathematical proportions recurred frequently in the natural world. Modern science has revealed to us a world of repeated shapes and patterns which appear to express some kind of unity for all things. We are part of this unity and perhaps, as the Greeks recognized, have an intuitive response to the natural laws governing harmony, rhythm, proportion, and balance.

Aesthetic education helps us to recognize true beauty which is never found in isolation. A tiger is more beautiful in its own habitat than when performing in a circus since its full beauty is seen only when a good relationship exists between it and its surroundings. Similarly, relationships exist between inanimate objects—things as mundane as a knife on a plate or a jug on a table. Put the knife in the jug and we are immediately aware of an incongruity. Obviously, this particular relationship is based on function, but not all relationships are so based. Shape, form, texture, colour, and sound may all serve as their base.

It may be easy, at this point, to fall into the trap of admiring a watered-down, over-sentimentalized beauty. The pastoral scene is attractive, but the man on the factory floor must relate to his work just as much as the farmer in his field. Is the relationship beautiful? It may be. Those of us who grew up in big cities or industrial areas may feel an instinctive love of the grimy buildings or the industrial dereliction, and we have this intuitive response even when our intellect tells us that the clean open spaces of the countryside are better. We respond in this way because we have an intuitive perception of the link between those places and the men who created them. All the elements of our humanity are there, good and bad—the creative pride of the men who invented the machines, the grim determination of the men and women whose lives were consequently enslaved contrasting with the blindness and inhumanity of those whose greed destroyed the environment and their fellow-men. Under normal circumstances we do not analyse in this way; it would be superfluous. It is sufficient that we feel it.

The artist not only feels it, he expresses it. Art critic Mervyn Levy wrote this about Theodore Major, a Lancashire painter: 'Major has found, in the grim surroundings of the industrial north, the perfect soil from which to forge his powerful, yet immensely subtle, poetic and often tender vision of the spiritual harmony which exists between man and the destiny of his surroundings.' Theodore Major himself wrote: 'I have seen where a white sun, a canal, a man looming out of the mist, could express a loveliness as wonderful as a wild flower in its setting.'

An artist such as Major devotes himself to the study and expression of people-environment relationships and so reveals spiritual values. He does not merely record or copy nature, for each of his paintings represents a question and, it is hoped, an answer. He must be bold enough to destroy the outward, surface appearance of nature in his quest to create and develop a new understanding. A photographic representation may be boring. We need the artist to say more. A reflection can never equal the object itself.

Some artists, not only painters, believe that the answer to life itself already exists, not outside man but within his own world of spirit and thought. Each great creative artist reveals a little more of this meaning, a little more of the beauty of existence, and of spiritual values. All truths are both permanent and eternal. They await the revelation of the artist, and when a truth finds expression, it brings with it a strange and moving beauty. High-flown thoughts perhaps. Interesting, maybe. But how, if at all, do they relate to the daily routine of the geography room?

Art in the geography classroom

It appears in no way strange, when discussing the teaching of geography, to mention people and environments and suggest that the ways in which people perceive and treat other people and environments reflect the goals that are implicit (though not necessarily explicit) within their culture.

Geography inevitably leads us to question whether such attitudes are moral, immoral, or amoral and requires us to recognize the role of aesthetic education in fostering the ability to make value judgements. Industrial man now has the ability to destroy his world by nuclear war, global pollution, or catastrophe of a different sort. Is his present disregard for the environment evil or stupid or is man in the end to be trusted? The inevitable questions which arise in our lessons are not specifically geographical and were being discussed long before the geography curriculum was invented.

Environmental and social issues have become commonplace in the geography room and by their nature raise moral and political questions. Politics comes into the implementation of decisions, but the decisions themselves ought not to be political. They must be based on spiritual values. Amongst those who deal with the spirit are the artists and more obviously, perhaps, the great religious teachers. I have, so far, avoided mentioning religion in this context, but it seems to me that the fundamental tenets of great art and great religions are the same. The problem with the latter is that all sorts of social factors accrue and blur the issue for those of different persuasions. Yet in the end terminology is of no importance.

I have also delayed mention of specific teaching situations because I believe them to be of lesser importance than the principles which govern them. Heaven knows that any teacher, arriving home tired after a day's work in the classroom and with domestic chores to be done (because that is the reality for most schoolteachers), would have the greatest difficulty perusing even a fraction of all the geography material published in the last few years. Who needs more? In some ways I believe that the obsession with curriculum planning has weakened the prospects for high-quality education. Some teachers have come to believe that the discovery of some magic curriculum will eliminate all the frustrations of the classroom. But the truth is that the best resource is a sensitive teacher.

For all our new methods—statistics, network analysis, games, simulations, and quantitative techniques—are we not still trying to sell the same package as before? Admittedly, it has been thinly disguised by a brighter, more exciting wrapping, but isn't it still the same old bundle of facts and figures? There may be some genuine enthusiasm and reward for both pupil and teacher in mastering the appropriate methods and techniques, but this hardly inspires or even touches that part of the mind with which true education should be concerned. The rationality which pervades so much of our teaching leads to a neglect of those qualities of intuition which provide the only real basis of human experience—harmony, rhythm, proportion, balance, and symmetry.

So what can the geography teacher do? How can he begin to cultivate aesthetic awareness, imagination, and intuition? Many must begin by acknowledging that their own education has ill-prepared them for such a role. Few are alive to quality and beauty in architecture and landscape, are visually literate or sensitive to the importance of shape, tone, colour, or style.

Such lack of awareness causes us to present the suffering and anguish of Third World problems in the form of population pyramids, bar graphs, or comprehension exercises. We speak of a technological crisis when the real crisis is within man himself. We think in terms of recording facts and ideas when we should be concerned with values and responses. To describe the problems and suggested, possible solutions is not enough.

I have, with some success, begun Third World studies with Beethoven's *Grosse Fuge* and with readings from Blake ('Desolation' from *The Four Zoas*). I have shown children how, in the fifteenth century, Hieronymus Bosch made beautiful but terrifying comment on the human condition in his paintings—

the *Garden of Earthly Delights* and the *Ship of Fools.* I have been more than pleased at the way in which children have thoughtfully responded after contrasting the vision of Michelangelo's David with the reality of poor, starved bodies, sick minds, unhappy households, and divided societies armed with terrible weapons.

How can we reconcile the children of Blake's *Songs of Innocence* with those half dead from hunger? Through an aesthetic approach pupils may be stimulated to see relevance in their prescribed studies and to feel a desire for involvement in other human lives. Possibly we can provoke a search for ultimate meaning leading to the realization that many aspects of life remain a mystery that we must continually strive to unfold.

For the geographer, there is relevance wherever man's creative spirit illuminates the human predicament on a fragile planet. The teacher need not, indeed must not, be afraid that he or she is unable or unqualified to expound upon music, painting, architecture or literature. I have used the late Beethoven quartets, the Mozart Clarinet Quintet, Bach's magnificent B Minor Mass; the poetry of Keats, Owen, Blake, Wordsworth, Clare; the paintings of Rembrandt, Chagall, Turner, Bruegel; and extracts from Solzhenitsyn, Joseph Heller, and D. H. Lawrence. It is better that great art be allowed to speak for itself.

The fact that Bosch in the fifteenth century could produce comment which is still relevant today suggests that the perception of human crises is long-established and not dependent upon more recent developments. His comment does not reduce horrors to lines on graphs or mere statistics.

Aesthetics and fieldwork

Fieldwork or local study has rightly established itself in geography at all levels and there are many excellent handbooks on fieldwork techniques. If data, maps, and photographs are provided in the classroom, it is quite possible to employ field techniques without leaving the classroom. What is vital to fieldwork is the hope that something rubs off, that there is an experience beyond that gained by using the secondary sources. Yet it seems that this experience is of minor importance to many teachers in terms of the discussion or writing they encourage. Rarely is there an attempt to give meaning to it, even though for most children the experience of the visit itself is far more important than the writing up.

For the past few years I have taken children to the small Bedfordshire village of Clophill. Throughout the period our resources have grown until there are now photographs, maps of all scales and types, prepared field sketches, worksheets, and hypotheses to test. Field techniques have included mapping buildings according to age, style, and materials. Much time has been spent on identifying styles from Queen Anne to the present day, and the pupils have learnt how to present this information graphically on bar charts, line graphs, maps, Venn diagrams, and the like. We identified stages of growth, saw the effect of break of slope on land use and vegetation, and determined how the shape or plan of the village had been governed by physical features. In short, the whole repertoire of fieldwork techniques was focused on this tiny village—yet its essence remained hidden. We made no mention of its gentle light, the beauty of pink, lavender and golden brick, the local stone, the gentle curves, and its Delft-like stillness and tranquillity. The feelings we had experienced during our visits could not be quantified or analysed. We were falling into the trap of classifying too much and enjoying too little.

Children had loved the place and this became the experience to tap. Suddenly it seemed obvious and easy to point out the poetry in buildings, their relationship to colour, sky, field, and trees. We noticed how the strength and maleness of Georgian buildings contrasted with the delicate and feminine Regency styles; how the relationship of glazing bars to glass was different, how the set of the windows (deeper in the Georgian style) and the respective roofscapes spoke differently. Victorian indulgence and opulence contrasted with the cool and classical. Mists and ploughed fields of autumn presented a different face from the clearer, more brittle light of spring when the cherry blossom became more important than the street furniture. The changes in light, shape, and tone as trees and buildings threw shadows became more important than questionnaires asking who shopped where, or 'Do you like living in your village?' Instead, it seemed important to ask, 'Do these new buildings "agree" with the rest? Do those? Does that? What about the "new" church (non-conformist 1920s)? Does Mill Lane feel different from the Broadway? Can we work out why?'

In the same way that the sound and spacing of words in poetry intensify feeling as well as meaning, so too do the form and setting of a building. We looked at fine ashlar work, various patterns of dripstones, string courses, and the rhythmic frieze of dentils which punctuate some fine examples of eighteenth and nineteenth century homes. We appreciated the way in which a building rendered in peach-pink stucco with white-painted sash windows relieved the monotony of brick and how the pale flettons (never intended as a facing brick) looked washed out. We became aware of how weathered bricks improve in appearance with age as do fine stone buildings (until advanced stages cause them to lose their sharpness), and of how plastic and concrete do not mature in this way at all. We learned how, with the invention of better methods of sheet-glass production, it became the fashion to omit glazing bars, making windows expressionless. The Victorian alternative is hardly better—a single bar down the centre. We all felt that glazing bars add much to the character of a house, both inside and out. The possibilities are endless.

Such discussions in the field lead to similar debates in the classroom. Is the Chinese collective farm really more relevant than pictures of the Sung landscapists? Surely to look at both will lead us to a deeper understanding of China and its people. Has the strange and wonderful architecture of the Middle East no place in our studies? How terrible to look upon a section of our world only as a faction in an ideological struggle or as a factor in the oil-supply situation. This is surely viewing through the wrong end of the telescope.

Conclusion

Art is man's reflection of his life and the world. It is a comment on what is and a pointer to what might be. If we ignore it, we ignore our own possibilities and are responsible for the lack of feeling and the greyness which threaten us.

The problem is partly historical. The Industrial Revolution brought a break with the past. Great machines destroyed one environment and created another. The tradition of craftsmen sympathetic to the materials they used and the forms they created has gone and, though we have learned to exert some influence or control over our surroundings, the process of destruction and re-creation continues at a faster pace. We have lost the ability to judge the things we make and the things we do, so that not only do we find ourselves surrounded by ugliness, but also bewildered by our situation. We are not involved in the things which control our lives and the alienation is illustrated daily in our schools.

What then can we do about the problems of an increasingly divided world? It would seem more important than ever that we seek and find the basic laws which govern our world for our surroundings leave a deep and lasting impression on us all.

Further reading

J. Berger, *Ways of Seeing* (Penguin, 1972).

K. Clark, *Landscape into Art* (John Murray, 1976).

G. Cullen, *Townscape* (Architectural Press, 1977).

M. Drabble, *A Writer's Britain: Landscape in Literature* (Thames & Hudson, 1979).

G. Grigson (ed.), *Poems and Places* (Faber, 1980).

J. Nellist, *British Architecture and its Background* (Macmillan, 1967).

D. Pocock (ed.) *Humanistic Geography and Literature* (Croom Helm, 1981).

H. Read, *Education through Art* (Faber, 1958).

The following issues of *Bulletin of Environmental Education* provide an introduction to the Schools Council Art and the Built Environment Project: 68 (1976); 72, 73 and 78 (1977); 83 (1978); 96 (1979).

Chapter 6

Welfare approaches to geography

John Bale

This chapter seeks to introduce the welfare approach to geography and suggest certain related teaching strategies for use at secondary school level.

Growing dissatisfaction with the inability of a quantitative and model-based geography to solve society's most pressing social problems led geographers in the early 1970s to question the relevance of their trade. The continued existence of the ghetto, neo-colonialism, urban crime, the negative impacts of growth (e.g. pollution) plus a recognition of the impersonal and sterile nature of much of the quantitative work contributed to a 'general feeling that the discipline was failing to respond to contemporary social issues'.[1]

At the same time welfare economics had been perceived as an alternative to micro-economics as a basis for location theory. Chisholm pointed out, for example, that it is important to distinguish between a situation which is optimal from a firm's viewpoint and that which represents a social optimum.[2] One result of these dissatisfactions has been the emergence of an approach to human geography, which culminated in the publication in 1977 of D. M. Smith's *Human Geography: A Welfare Approach*. In addition a number of publications have emerged dealing with individual areas of social concern. The McGraw-Hill series titled *Problems in Geography* includes coverage of subjects like the ghetto, crime and justice, health care, urban politics, and atmospheric pollution. The subject matter of these books includes some areas in which geographers had traditionally shown little concern and others where the focus of attention had traditionally been more academic than applied.

The title of Smith's book is significant for he does not call it 'welfare geography'. This would simply be another variety of adjectival geography to add to the fifty-seven (or more) other varieties. Instead Smith avers that because the whole of human geography is pervaded by issues of human and social well-being, the employment of the welfare theme actually defines a *new* human geography. Welfare is roughly synonymous with well-being, satisfaction, happiness, quality of life, real income, and other cognate terms. Essentially, a welfare approach focuses on the study of who gets what where. Obviously the most geographical aspect of this phrase is 'where', but the question of 'who' certainly includes consideration of the size or nature of the areal units being studied while 'how' involves understanding the dynamics (including those of a spatial nature) by which particular patterns emerge. The 'what' question involves a problem of deciding exactly what it is which gives people satisfaction and well-being—a subject having profound geographical implications in a world of limitless wants and finite resources.

The model-based paradigm and the application of quantitative methods are in no way in conflict with the welfare approach. Indeed, it has been argued that the challenge to contemporary geography is not to overthrow positivism but 'to design an education which combines the technical strength of the quantitative and model-building era with a passionate concern for the condition of mankind'.[3] Hence well-known models and statistical techniques are in no way jettisoned but are modified or applied in a more socially relevant form. For example, Lösch's demand cone becomes an externality cone; von Thünen is used to explain, not the location of crops, but of slums; Weber's distance-minimizing industrial location model is converted into Smith's least-distance maternity hospital location model—expectant mothers rather than iron ore being the 'quantities' transported. Urban hierarchies are recipients, not of conventional kinds of innovations, but of capital flows in the process of colonization. Scattergraphs, Lorenz curves, computer-drawn maps, and statistical formulae litter Smith's text. The spatial paradigm prevails, but it is a spatial welfare approach or what another Smith called 'a seemingly benevolent positivism'.[4] The concern remains with normative models—models which tell us what *ought* to be rather than what is. But the criteria used and the assumptions made in arriving at these models are those which maximize social well-being rather than profits.

Knowledge about socially relevant phenomena is portrayed geographically in map form. Social data, when mapped, often produce single-feature regions, and regional geography can be regarded as very much alive since in a welfare approach it becomes the 'analysis of who gets what where in a specific territorial context'.[5] Little or no prescription for political change is found in the welfare geographic approach. The emphasis tends to be on locational adjustments to society's ills, and in this sense it should be described as liberal rather than radical in outlook. Simply applying geographical skills to relevant matters and oppressed peoples does not involve questioning the contradictions of western capitalism, but in the USA, at least, the welfare movement paved the way for a more revolutionary form of geography.[6]

Examples of three approaches

Three approaches seem to have characterized work which can be broadly included under the social-welfare umbrella. First, there has been a concern with describing geographically (i.e. mapping) patterns of welfare at a variety of geographic scales, ranging from global through national and regional to local levels. At the same time there have been many studies which *describe* regional variations in one specific topical area of the discipline, for example, geographical variations in schizophrenia, alcoholism, juvenile delinquency, and sub-standard housing. Variation in provision of goods such as swimming pools, sports centres, and golf courses has also been analysed. A second approach is one which tries to *understand* the patterns of welfare revealed cartographically. This involves not only the application of various models but also an awareness of a newly emergent and transformed political geography.[7] A third and final approach would be to *predict* a more socially just pattern of welfare.

While it is inevitable that inequality in access will exist (in as much as everybody cannot be in the same place at the same time), this inequality of access to basic services and facilities can be minimized. Likewise, inequality in welfare can be reduced, though the means of doing so are obviously open to fierce debate. The intention of the remainder of this chapter is to illustrate examples of each of these three approaches and to exemplify their translation to classroom strategies at secondary school level. It can be argued that an infusion of welfare approaches to school geography will in no way reduce the rigour of the hard-fought revolution of recent decades, but it will add a degree of relevance, humanism, and political education to already well-tried approaches.

i) *Describing patterns of welfare*

Before illustrating methods of describing regional differences in well-being, it is important to point out that there is a considerable difference in opinion regarding how welfare can be maximized. For example, should society work towards a more equal regional distribution of welfare (the Lorenz criterion) or is welfare improved if some regions get richer without others getting poorer (the Pareto criterion)? In addition, what indicators should be used in order to arrive at some operational definition of welfare? Since there is no generally accepted list of criteria which go to make up well-being, a large number of variables ranging from protein intake to footwear consumption and from the beauty of the environment to teacher-pupil ratios have been used. In a study of spatial variations in the quality of life in England and Wales, Knox employed fifty-three variables in order to arrive at an overall level of living index.[8]

An important pedagogic aim of studies which try to identify the quality of life is that of diverting students away from the view that gross national product or national income figures are the sole indicators of development or well-being and that after GNP per capita reaches a critical level, the rate of increase in the quality of life begins to slow down. Indeed, it has been suggested that there might actually be negative returns to further increases in material affluence.[9] The use of an index rather than simply a per capita GNP figure can be applied at the school level in several ways. Westaway illustrates an approach used by sixth-form students which involves discussion of which kinds of variables should be used, the simple calculation of a composite index of development, and a consideration of the limitations of the methods used.[10] Smallbone has illustrated a useful method of arriving at a level of living index for the standard regions of Britain.[11]

At the simplest level, middle school students could arrive at a simple composite index by summing the ranks of regions on a number of variables, the region with the lowest sum of ranks having the highest overall quality of life or level of living. A more sophisticated approach used with undergraduate students and incorporating a weighting procedure to include group value judgements about the relative importance of the different variables used has been discussed by Smith.[12] These exercises may be undertaken from the local to international scale. Being aimed at different levels of the educational hierarchy, the concept of level of living can be used in the classroom in structured, progressive courses so that the concept is returned to at increasing levels of complexity. At the same time it needs to be accepted that the indicators used in arriving at a composite index are strongly biased towards quantifiable material criteria, often culturally derived.

The identification of regional variations in individual socially relevant phenomena may also be undertaken in schools from secondary or primary materials. Telephone directories, land-use maps, and local newspapers reveal rich data on local variations in the provision of doctors, derelict land, and other benefits and nuisances of the urban scene. The mapped patterns of such phenomena will bring home to students the regional inequality in provision; if population figures and ward boundaries are also available, per capita figures could easily be calculated. The vast potential for street work is highlighted by Bunge's provocative work in Detroit and Toronto.[13] Maps displaying such readily gathered data as areas inaccessible to parkland, abandoned buildings, litter, and other such variables would be easy for children to collect. Yet as Storm pointed out over a decade ago, it is frequently easier for the teacher to avoid talking about such local issues and simply distribute a set of textbooks and talk about coffee in Brazil.[14]

A major concept within the welfare approach is that of the proximity of certain groups of people to facilities which generate spillover effects (or externalities). The most well-known examples of negative externalities are pollutants, the effects of which usually display a well-marked distance decay pattern. The geographic expression of such spillovers is the externality field. A work unit on this subject has been outlined by Bale[15] and a fieldwork approach produced by Hammond.[16] An attempt which seeks to delimit perceived negative externality fields is illustrated in Figure 9, in this case the perceived nuisance effects of two football clubs. At each point shown on the maps residents were asked if they found the football club (i) a serious nuisance, (ii) a nuisance, or (iii) no nuisance at all. Each point was scored 2, 1 or 0 respectively, and nuisance contours interpolated.[17] This kind of work can be undertaken from the fourth year of the secondary school, modifications being added depending on the level and ability of the students.

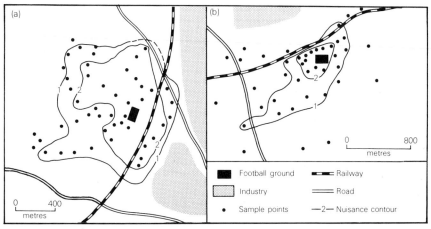

Fig. 9   The nuisance fields of (a) Derby County and (b) Charlton Athletic football clubs. Nuisance contours delimit areas over which the football club is perceived by local residents as (1) a nuisance and (2) a severe nuisance

In each of the examples discussed so far it is obvious that some people are disadvantaged solely on the basis of where they happen to live or were born. The full impact of such studies would be achieved if students could empathize with the disadvantaged groups. Such empathy is more likely to be achieved, however, if an understanding of the processes giving rise to inequality are considered. This forms the subject matter of the next section.

ii) Towards an understanding of patterns of welfare

Having identified the kinds of problems encountered in the welfare approach, we may briefly consider some ways in which such inequalities arise. In large measure inequalities in provision of various facilities, accessibility, and well-being can be accounted for by the exercise of *power* of one group over another. Implicit in this concern with power is the view that a new political geography might emerge where the importance of political decisions on spatial distributions extended beyond the traditional themes of government policy on industrial location and the like. Putting it bluntly, Johnston writes: 'Why bother school children with the rank size rule, or any so-called laws of location; much more relevant is the basic political law—"get power and then hang onto it"—which has many spatial ramifications'.[18]

The growing geographical interest in power has taken a variety of forms, few of which have been explicitly diffused at school level. There is a need to employ a number of studies in both the USA and Britain which have considered the role of the property market, for example, in the exercise of power in the allocation of housing. In studies of the so-called Third World the covert power held by multinational corporations and spatial discrimination adopted by their investment policies have been highlighted. The way in which the occident continues to exploit the orient reflects another example of power at the global scale. From a pedagogic standpoint the concept of power can be incorporated by giving greater stress to the role of the various agencies which constrain locational choices at varying levels of scale. For example, Ambrose and Colenutt have argued that the school curriculum ought to give greater emphasis to such questions as 'why are some people without a home?', 'who owns the centre of our town?', or 'who decided that the marina should be built?'. These questions are conceptually no more difficult than many others raised in the early years of the secondary school yet children enter the outside world often knowing more about Hadrian's Wall than the locational policies of building societies.[19]

At the practical level the concept of power can probably be best taught from a gaming approach. While it is true that an understanding of conflict may be achieved from role-play approaches, the fact that students are acting out other people's lives reduces the impact of the game. Approaches such as those adopted in the game Starpower,[20] on the other hand, involve things actually happening to people in the room—the players themselves. Starpower does present some problems with students below the age of about eighteen and for this reason a simpler game, devised by Neubeck, can be used.[21] In this game the teacher proceeds by giving the class a general knowledge test, constructed in such a way that a wide range of marks should result. It is also important that the teacher gives the test before the class is fully assembled. As late members of the class assemble they take the test like everybody else but they are not allowed to re-take the questions they missed through lateness. Following the test, individuals' scores are compared; the range of marks is noted; the question of whether it was 'fair' that those who came in late should be deprived of marks can be raised. It might be suggested that the marks obtained for the test represent earned income. Should people who failed to get in for the start of the test (through no fault of their own in some cases) get a lower mark than those who were in the room throughout? Could class marks be raised if co-operation had been allowed? What if each student represents a region? The welfare implications and the arbitrariness of the variations in 'income' should be obvious. How should the total income be distributed among individuals? The real-world analogues will be obvious.

iii) Predicting better patterns of welfare
A characteristic of recent work in geography has been the application of sophisticated computer models to the solution of welfare questions. One of the main aims of optimizing models is to maximize equity by selecting locations for public services which reduce the longest journey of any consumer to a minimum. This approach accords, of course, with Christaller's central place theory. Hodgart quotes the interesting example of where to locate a new swimming pool in a city.[22] He notes that in the case of Edinburgh, 'aggregate travel to the present pools is 42 per cent greater than to the optimal locations' and argues that the newest pool was wrongly located in an area of the city already well served (Figure 10).

It is possible with the growth of micro-computers in schools and the

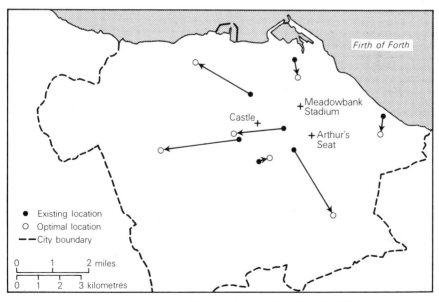

Fig. 10   Comparison of actual locations of public swimming pools in Edinburgh in 1971 with locations which minimize aggregate travel (source: Hodgart, ref. 22)

LAMBETH: SWIMMING POOLS—ACCESSIBILITY

National surveys indicate that swimming has a wide appeal for all age groups. A high number of participants are frustrated by a lack of accessible facilities. A recent questionnaire survey carried out in Lambeth found that 66 per cent of users of swimming pools travel less than one mile to a pool.

Let us discover just how much of Lambeth is not properly served by existing or proposed swimming pools. (See map, Fig. 12.)

1 Using a compass draw a circle one mile wide around the existing swimming pools.
2 Shade in the area *not served* by a pool lightly in red.
3 Now draw a circle (*in blue pencil*) one mile around the proposed swimming pools.

IN YOUR EXERCISE BOOKS ANSWER THESE QUESTIONS

1 How far do most swimming pool users travel to swim?
2 How many pools at present serve Lambeth? Which of these are not in the borough?
3 How many more pools are proposed?
4 Which area is at present not served by pools?
5 Approximately how large is this area?
6 Which area will still not be served by pools even after the proposed pools have been built?
7 Approximately how large is this area?
8 If you could build one more new pool where would you build it? Mark it on your map and key.
9 Explain why you chose this location.

Fig. 11 *Worksheet for an exercise on predicting the most equitable location for a new swimming pool in Lambeth (source: Darby, ref. 24)*

growing involvement of geography teachers with developments in computer education[23] that optimizing models of the type used in studies such as that described above will be used in schools. Already, applications of the Weber model exist and as was discussed above, the basic Weber principle can be readily applied to welfare questions.

More likely, however, are classroom approaches which attempt to identify gaps in provision of particular facilities and then simulate a revised, more equitable, pattern. A large number of these kinds of simulations exist and basically they involve students in selecting a location from several alternatives and justifying their final choice. A good example of this approach involved fourth-year students in inner London identifying the catchment areas of existing and proposed swimming pools in Lambeth and then predicting the best location for a new pool (Figures 11 and 12).[24] Although very simple, the underlying aim of the exercise is clearly to highlight inequality of provision and work towards a more equitable distribution of facilities.

It is not difficult to think of a large number of other facilities which could replace swimming pools in the above example. The question of accessibility, one which has interested both geographers and educators in geography for some time, should not be ignored in our classrooms in an era of the thinning out of low order services and the centralizing of facilities at fewer points. Work on accessibility problems in rural areas needs early translation into pedagogic strategies so that children might realize the negative impacts of the rationalization of facility provision.

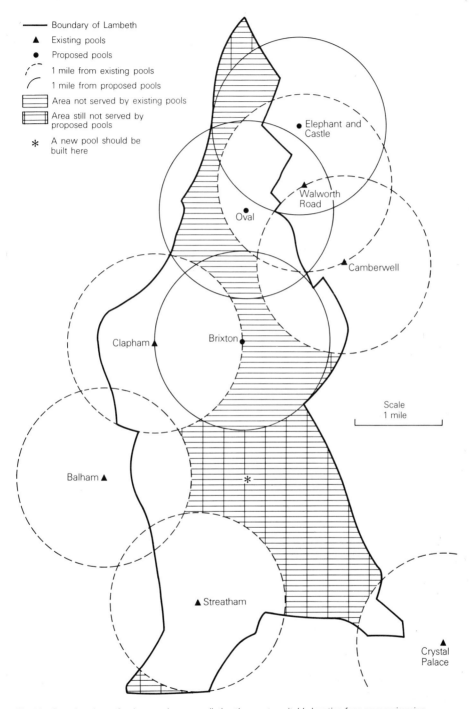

Legend:
- —— Boundary of Lambeth
- ▲ Existing pools
- ● Proposed pools
- ⌐ 1 mile from existing pools
- ⌐ 1 mile from proposed pools
- ▤ Area not served by existing pools
- ▦ Area still not served by proposed pools
- ＊ A new pool should be built here

Fig. 12   Completed map for the exercise on predicting the most equitable location for a new swimming pool in Lambeth (source: Darby, ref. 24)

Conclusion and implications

Welfare approaches to human geography have emerged as a response to the excesses of the scientific mood of the 1960s. Much of what has been described in this chapter has been far from revolutionary. A welfare approach builds on the gains of the previous decades and might best be described as liberal in orientation. Because it sees spatial change occurring within the existing political system, a welfare focus would seem to be more attractive to many school teachers than a radical alternative. Forer and Owens argue that 'radicalism and Marxism are perhaps rather difficult to bring into the school situation, at least in anything but the most watered-down sense. Social justice is more suited to bring into school geography. The notions of equity and equal distribution (e.g. of facilities in space) or questions about regional balance and prosperity seem valuable concepts for the classroom'.[25] The welfare approach builds on the positivist experience of young geography teachers rather than replacing it with alternative paradigms. Culture shock is therefore avoided, or at least reduced, for under the liberal umbrella human geography remains normative in nature.

Yet problems remain for teachers espousing the liberal-welfare approach. The welfare approach offers 'no serious solution to the problem that self-interested acquisitiveness poses for social order and environmental integrity'.[26] Solutions are usually seen as operating within an essentially growth-oriented ethos. By no means unrelated to this ethos is the practical classroom problem of continuing to allow the examination 'tail' to wag the curriculum 'dog'.

If the end purpose of a liberal geography becomes the passing of examinations, its essentially humanistic leanings will disappear. It is essential, therefore, that content changes in the geography curriculum should not occur in isolation from more humanistic modes of pedagogy. A geography including a real concern for variations in the quality of life is a relevant but not a revolutionary geography. At worst, its widespread adoption would make school geography more appropriate to the world in which our children will live; at best it might point the way towards Bunge's world of 'happy regions'.

References

1   D. M. Smith, *Human Geography: a Welfare Approach* (Arnold, 1977), p. 4.
2   M. Chisholm, 'In search of a basis for location theory: micro-economics or welfare economics?', *Progress in Geography*, 3 (1971), pp. 111–33.
3   D. M. Smith, 'Who gets what *where,* and how: a welfare focus for human geography', *Geography*, 59 (1974), p. 297.
4   N. Smith, 'Geography, science and post-positivist modes of explanation', *Progress in Human Geography*, 3 (1979), p. 375.
5   D. M. Smith, op. cit. (ref. 1), p. 13.
6   R. Peet (ed.), *Radical Geography* (Methuen, 1977).
7   K. Cox, *Location and Public Problems* (Blackwell, 1979)

8   P. Knox, 'Spatial variations in the level of living in England and Wales', *Transactions*, Institute of British Geographers, 62 (1974).

9   D. M. Smith, op. cit. (ref. 1), p. 221.

10   J. Westaway, 'Measuring development', *Teaching Geography*, 5, 4 (1980), pp. 165–7.

11   D. Smallbone, 'Measuring regional imbalance', *Classroom Geographer* (Oct. 1977), pp. 7–13.

12   D. M. Smith, 'The welfare approach to human geography', *Values, Relevance and Policy* (Open University, Course D204), pp. 22–8.

13   W. Bunge and R. Bordessa, *The Canadian Alternative* (York University, Toronto, 1975).

14   M. Storm, 'Teaching about the community: an issue-based approach', in J. Bale, N. Graves and R. Walford (eds.), *Perspectives in Geographical Education* (Oliver & Boyd, 1973).

15   J. Bale, 'Teaching welfare issues in urban geography', in R. Walford (ed.), *Signposts for Geography Teaching* (Longman, 1981).

16   R. Hammond, 'Externalities: the benefits and problems of where you live', *Teaching Geography*, 4, 2 (1978), pp. 68–70.

17   J. Bale, 'Football clubs as neighbours', *Town and Country Planning*, 49, 3 (1980).

18   R. J. Johnston, 'On geography and the organization of education', *Journal of Geography in Higher Education*, 1 (1977), pp. 5–12.

19   P. Ambrose and R. Colenutt, *The Property Machine* (Penguin, 1975), p. 184.

20   G. Shirts, *Starpower* (Western Behavioral Sciences Institute, 1969).

21   K. Neubeck, 'An income distribution simulation', in D. J. Whitehead (ed.), *Handbook for Economics Teachers* (Heinemann, 1979), pp. 264–6.

22   R. Hodgart, 'Optimizing access to public services', *Progress in Human Geography*, 2, 1 (1978), pp. 17–48.

23   I. Shepherd, Z. Cooper and D. Walker, *Computer Assisted Learning in Geography* (Council for Educational Technology/Geographical Association, 1980).

24   H. Darby, 'An introduction to accessibility and leisure through local swimming pool provision', *Classroom Geographer* (March 1978), pp. 22–4.

25   P. Forer and I. F. Owens, 'The frontiers of geography in the 1980s', *New Zealand Journal of Geography*, 67 (1979), pp. 2–5.

26   I. Wallace, 'Towards a humanized conception of economic geography', in D. Ley and M. Samuels (eds.), *Humanistic Geography* (Croom Helm, 1975), p. 105.

Further reading

B. Coates, R. Johnston and P. Knox, *Geography and Inequality* (OUP, 1977).

E. Jones and J. Eyles, *An Introduction to Social Geography* (OUP, 1977).

M. Moseley, *Accessibility: the Rural Challenge* (Methuen, 1979).

D. M. Smith, *Where the Grass is Greener* (Penguin, 1979).

Chapter 7

Radical geography

Ian Cook

This chapter describes the development of radical geography and shows how its growth can be related to the wider social and historical context in which the subject developed. A brief introduction to the Marxist and anarchist approaches which underpin radical methodology is then given via a critique of *People, Place and Work* (GYSL/Avery Hill 14–16 Project). In this way several alternatives to the traditional curricula are sketched out in order to suggest the directions in which a truly concerned and committed radical geography might develop in schools.

The first radical geographers can be said to be the nineteenth century geographers (and anarchists) Elisée Reclus and Peter Kropotkin. Reclus's *Nouvelle Géographie Universelle* was recently described as being 'distinguished by its broad humanity as well as by its comprehensiveness',[1] while Kropotkin's article in the journal *The Nineteenth Century*, entitled 'What geography ought to be' provides 'a passionate and deeply humane statement of the social significance of a geographical education'.[2] It is a damning indictment of the subject that the work of both these men, highly respected during their lifetimes, was ignored until recently. Indeed, various authors have mistakenly suggested that the first radical geographers were either Jean Brunhes, the French geographer, the British tropical geographers of the 1930s and after, or various geographers working in the United States from the mid 1960s.

Nonetheless it was in North America that radical geography was reborn. In 1969 the radical geography journal, *Antipode*, was founded at Clark University, Worcester, Massachusetts and the Union of Socialist Geographers was established in Toronto in 1974. A British branch was not created until 1978 at the annual conference of the Institute of British Geographers in Hull.

The development of radical geography in North America can only be understood by relating it to the broader social tensions within North American society. For example, the civil rights movement was raising fundamental questions concerning racial inequalities, while the Vietnam war with its catalogue of horrors was raising fundamental questions concerning the ethics of a society which could utilize technological achievements to such ends as napalm bombing, defoliation, and destruction. Many academics found themselves being forced for the first time to question seriously their own role in reproducing such a society and were radicalized as a result. The conservative nature of American universities, their involvement with big business and the federal government, and the pressures put upon staff to undertake research for such institutions (with all the implications for reducing academic freedom) also fostered radicalism.

Such tensions were exacerbated for many geographers by a strong disillusionment with the new geography of positivism (Chapter 14). Those who believed that geography should be a live subject concerned with relevant social and environmental issues had powerful reasons to develop a critique of the depersonalization and depoliticization of their subject. Their critique found expression in various ways. For example, Bill Bunge, well known for his earlier innovative textbook on theoretical geography, set up and led a series of geographical expeditions into depressed urban areas. Focusing upon Detroit, Toronto, and Windsor (Ontario), they were designed as:

> 'an attempt to get radical geography as a whole moving . . . to
> supply people in a community with information and tools to fight
> conditions of poverty and deprivation . . . to break down the
> division between scholarly work and fieldwork and between the
> professional geographer and the folk geographer (the latter a
> community resident having access to training and information
> provided by field workers). Expeditions were seen as valuable in that
> they forced middle-class professionals to realize problems which
> they could never have perceived as such, as a result of being forced to
> see an urban working-class community through the eyes of its
> residents.'[3]

The expeditions had a marked practical and activist focus which was regarded as being more important than the development of a deep theoretical understanding of the problems with which they dealt. Other radicals, however, were more concerned to construct the latter and therefore turned primarily to Marxism for the appropriate methodology, outlined more fully below. It can be noted here that Marxist geographers believe that spatial and environmental problems can only be understood via a realization that they result from the impact of capitalism upon society. Such geographers have begun to develop theoretical perspectives upon such problems as the inner city, regional inequalities, underdevelopment, and so on.[4] The contentious nature of these new perspectives meant that many of the geographical periodicals and journals were unwilling to publish such material, which led to the establishment of *Antipode*. This journal continues 'to ask value questions within geography, question existing institutions concerning their rates and qualities of change, and question the individual concerning his own commitments.'[5]

Based upon these two pillars of activism and theoretical development, radical geography has grown and is now making an impact upon the subject as a whole. Problems have of course arisen between the radicals and the geographical establishment, with the reaction of the latter taking one of two forms. Dissenting radicals are either co-opted and assimilated into the geographical hierarchy in an attempt to defuse their radicalism, or conversely are denied access to teaching posts and media of communication in an attempt to remove them from the subject itself. As a result of these processes radicals are often operating in difficult isolated conditions, but many find solidarity in the Union of Socialist Geographers.

'The purpose of our union is to work for the radical restructuring of our societies in accord with the principles of social justice. As geographers and as people we will contribute to this process in two complementary ways:
i) organizing and working for radical change in our communities, and
ii) developing geographic theory to contribute to revolutionary struggle.
Thus we subscribe to the principle: from each according to ability, to each according to need. We declare that the development of a humane, non-alienating society requires, as its most fundamental step, socialization of the means of production.'[6]

Brian Berry has commented about the USG, 'there's no more amusing thing than goading a series of malcontents and kooks and freaks and dropouts and so on, which is after all what that group mainly consists of. There are very few scholars in the group.'[7]

If radical geography is to be introduced into schools then it must be realized that similar comments and sanctions will face those teachers concerned to encourage it. It is easy to disparage radical geography as being non-academic or pure ideology, but radicals would contend that it is positivist geography that is ideological, and that good and relevant intellectual enquiry demands commitment and involvement in social problems. These contentions rest upon Marxist and anarchist perceptions of the social system which will now be outlined in order that the intellectual bases of radical geography can be understood.

A critique of People, Place and Work

While Marxism exists in many forms, most radical geographers adhere to neo-Marxism of the type associated with the New Left in Western Europe and North America since the mid 1950s. Neo-Marxists seek to overcome earlier dogmatism and develop a fully dynamic and evolving approach which facilitates a critique not only of advanced capitalist societies but also of those communist regimes which merely replace capitalism by a form of state capitalism rather than true socialism. Although it is Marxism which dominates radical geography, anarchist ideas should not be ignored because they provide a counterbalance to a preoccupation with theory at the expense of active involvement in contemporary social problems. Both approaches shall therefore be illustrated here.

People, Place and Work from the GYSL/Avery Hill 14–16 Project[8] will be used as the focal point around which examples of alternative perspectives will be given. The project represents a considerable advance over the type of geography studied previously, making a serious attempt to present relevant examples of the nature of work in modern society. Nonetheless it fails to explain adequately, even at a simple level, the real basis of work today, namely as a reflection of the needs of capitalism. In the text there is no explanation of the unfolding impact of capitalism upon different peoples, places, and environments, and it is essential that this process be dealt with, even at the ability level of the 14–16 year olds at whom the project is aimed. Without this explanation pupils will fail to understand their own society and other societies adequately, the shortcomings of their society will be glossed over, the status quo will be upheld through ignorance of alternatives, and there will be little informed dynamic for change and improvement. While this may well suit the needs of the state and of capitalism, it may not suit the needs of people in general. Society can only advance on the basis of informed and educated citizens, and geographers must not seek to avoid the issues raised by such an education.

In order that the nature of work can be understood it must be studied within its full social and historical context, for the work pattern in any place reflects the structure of the society which inhabits that place, the structure of the other societies which interact with it, and any specific factors unique to that place. The project fails to place its examples within the broader context, therefore the level of explanation is low. Further, an implicit acceptance of the status quo permeates much of the text, and there is little attempt at serious debate concerning alternatives to the work ethic or to the system which controls work itself. In parts, acceptance of the status quo is explicit rather than implicit. For example Rostow's outdated and unacceptable stages of growth model forms the basis for the all too brief section on the inter-national scale; the Drumbuie game refers to 'intelligent' and 'very clever' officials and other supporters of the development option, contrasting with the 'very excitable', 'very outspoken', 'noisiest and most argumentative' opponents of the scheme (one protester is 'a rather brusque person, much less pleasant than his wife'); while there is little reference to unemployment in the project, whenever it is discussed it is seen simply as a problem of technology versus labour rather than capital versus labour. Rather than dwell upon points of detail such as these, however, I shall sketch out the alternative framework in which work can be more readily understood. This framework could also be used for the examination of other topics within the Avery Hill Project.

An alternative approach to People, Place and Work

Work can only be understood via an understanding of capitalism. Capitalism is a particular form of human society which evolved from feudal society via mercantilism, a merchant-based society which concentrated upon the trade of goods produced by a variety of producers whose output was not readily controllable by the merchants themselves. With the development of capital-ism, output came increasingly under control as money was invested in labour rather than in goods and as capitalists developed large-scale factory production in order to increase vastly the amount of surplus value or profit which could be extracted from the workforce. Analysis of work should begin with examination of this process and of examples drawn from the eighteenth and nineteenth centuries to illustrate the changes wrought in this process.

It may be argued that examples drawn from this period lead us into the study of history rather than geography. Failure to appreciate the time dimension, however, would result in a geographical analysis which appeared to be dynamic in that as geographers we would concentrate upon spatial and environmental processes but which in fact would be static in time. The examples would of course have to be chosen in order to illustrate spatial and environmental themes, therefore they would have to describe the rapid transition from an agricultural society generally enjoying an intimate, small-scale interaction with its environment and place to an industrialized society generally alienated from its milieu.

From this perspective, therefore, it would seem that a study of work should provide examples such as the following, which are drawn from rural-urban, agricultural-industrial, and British-foreign dimensions. First, the life and work of a typical mid- to late- eighteenth-century farmworker would be described, highlighting such features as the influence of environmental factors upon his work pattern, the smallness of the world in which he lived and the low level of his material base. Landlord-tenant relationships, the nature and payment of rent, contrasting levels of wealth and poverty, and the life-chances of the farmworker and his family would also be referred to in order to illustrate the positive and negative aspects of his work situation in that place at that time. This situation would be placed in context by describing the growing impact of the Agricultural and Industrial Revolutions and the growing pressures forcing and encouraging the farmworker to leave the land, either for the embryonic industrial towns or for a new life in the colonies.

The second example would describe the dramatic contrast of the work of a Lancashire cotton worker in one of the 'dark Satanic mills' of the Industrial Revolution. Points to be made would include similarities with the first example in respect of the long hard hours worked, lack of leisure time, and the smallness of the factory worker's world. Contrasts would include the emphasis upon wage labour, the unseasonal and hence unnatural hours of employment (dictated by the rhythm of the clock rather than by nature), the pressures of working in a factory environment, the unattractive life in an early industrial town, and so on. The context would be provided by reference to the growing differentiation of society into workers (the proletariat) and employers (the capitalists). Examples could also be provided of the employment of women and children in order to focus upon the exploitation of human resources common in this period, and of the first stirrings of the working-classes in their efforts to organize and so combat such exploitation.

The broader impact of the Industrial Revolution would also be analysed. Themes to emerge might include the rapid rate of nineteenth-century urbanization, with the high levels of squalor, poverty, crime and disease, as well as the changing work patterns, the growth of the coalfields, and the concomitant development of the iron and steel industry, shipbuilding, and the railways. Should time permit, examples could be presented of the work of coalminers, foundry-workers, navvies and the like in order to illustrate the increasing specialization of work and contrasts between skilled and unskilled workers. The origins of the worker, the reasons for his migration to the industrial heartland, and the potential employment of his wife and children would also be worthy of examination in order to show how regional disparities were increasing in the capitalist system.

Disparities were also increasing at the international scale. Capitalism requires large and lucrative markets for its products so that surplus value can be realized, and also cheap human and natural resources to exploit elsewhere as it both uses up its indigenous natural resources and is faced by an increasingly organized indigenous workforce. In the nineteenth century these requirements manifested themselves as the era of colonialism, or more properly imperialism, with capital allying itself with the state to carve up the globe and ensure its own monopoly in specific areas. The process of imperialism can be regarded as providing the fuel for the capitalist engine as capital migrates across international boundaries in the ceaseless search for profit. In the nineteenth century British industry prospered at the expense of that in the colonies. Therefore it would be instructive to present an example of, say, an Indian cotton worker losing his employment as cotton goods were imported from the United Kingdom. Such an example would serve not only to explain the impact of British industry upon other areas but also to put contemporary arguments for protectionism into a wider perspective.

With reference to the twentieth century, themes which must be discussed are: the struggle for independence of the underdeveloped nations of the Third World (an independence which has seen many such countries free themselves from the political shackles imposed upon them by the imperialist powers, but not from the socio-economic shackles of neo-imperialism); the creation of the so-called 'second world' of the communist states; and the changing balance of power and wealth in the 'first world'. A study of work could illustrate these themes as follows. First, radical geographers believe that capitalism actively creates underdevelopment via its exploitation of Third World countries. Although certain benefits spin off from capital investment in Third World economies, this investment concentrates development into islands of export-oriented industries in seas of largely subsistence agricultural economies. The investment is mainly within the urban areas at the expense of the rural sectors, which lag further and further behind the pace of development in the cities. The resulting contrasts could be exemplified by comparing the work pattern of a peasant engaged in subsistence agriculture with an established former peasant working in, say, garment manufacturing in one of the primate cities of Asia or Latin America. The work of a recent migrant in the quasi-subsistence bazaar economy would also present an interesting comparison with these examples, examples which would help correct the ethnocentric bias found in *People, Place and Work*.

The birth of the communist states appeared to present dramatic alternatives to the work patterns of capitalist societies, but although contrasts undoubtedly exist so too do certain similarities. For example, the production-line system can alienate communist and capitalist worker alike as it dehumanizes the process of labour; investment is concentrated heavily in the large-scale, capital-intensive armaments and nuclear power industries which are similar in both systems; technology is placed in high regard; bureaucracies are also on the increase in both systems and the emphasis upon white-collar employment is common to both. The Marxist would tend to argue that these processes reflect the dominance of capitalism in the world system which has made it difficult for communist countries to pursue alternative policies as capitalism seeks to suppress them by military, or more subtly, by economic means. Also, the transition to socialism is long and difficult and state capitalism may be necessary en route, with the centralized state bureaucracy taking over the mode of production but running it largely on capitalist lines. Anarchists would be more critical of the role of the Party in this process and would suggest that it may seek to impose its own dictatorship rather than the dictatorship of the proletariat. Examples comparing the work of workers in a car factory in the Soviet Union and the United States, technicians in nuclear power plants or civil servants in contrasting capitalist and communist systems would aid discussion of these points, which are important in determining the direction in which society should evolve.

The third theme refers to the growth of the United States during the twentieth century and the rise of West Germany and Japan as highly advanced industrial nations in contrast to the comparative decline of, for example, the United Kingdom. These contrasting rates of growth are often attributed to the fact that 'they work harder', 'the trade unions are too powerful in the United Kingdom', and so on, oversimplistic viewpoints which ignore contrasting levels of capital investment, management training, the debts incurred by the lend-lease policy during the Second World War, the impact of the Marshall Plan, and the flight of capital from the peripheral regions of Britain. A project upon work must compare and contrast work patterns in such countries, and in so doing must seek to answer the questions of what is work for, and who it is for.

Increasingly people are working for big corporate bodies in which they have little control over their own labour. These bodies include the multinational and transnational corporations which treat international boundaries with disdain, and the state in all its ramifications including the local state, the machinery of local government, and the nationalized industries—the loss-making industries which capitalism is not too unhappy to discard. Comparisons of the blue-collar and white-collar workers in selected industries in contrasting countries must be made in order to evaluate the quality and worth of work in contemporary society.

Finally, in developing a curriculum of the type sketched here the geographer must attempt some analysis of the alternatives to the present system of work. As noted above, the problem is not simply one of technology versus labour, but rather of capital versus labour. Although capitalism has brought many material benefits in its wake, the emphasis upon the profit motive and competitiveness has brought many problems. For example, for many years the leisure boom has been anticipated and the microchip revolution, it is suggested, will at last bring this about. However, it seems more likely that working hours will not be cut across the board but that certain sectors of society will lose work altogether. Some estimates suggest that 50 million will be unemployed in Europe alone by the late 1980s. And yet this trend is concurrent with an United Nations estimate that 50 million children, mainly in Third World countries, are subject to the degradation of child labour. Surely we can evolve alternatives to the wastage of human resources which this entails. Such alternatives must develop from a decentralization and devolution of power and control in modern society to enable more people to have more control over their own labour and hence their own lives. A project upon work, therefore, should conclude with the examination of non-work, and the evaluation of communal forms of society in which work is relegated to its proper place, that is as a means to an end rather than as an end in itself.

Adoption of a radical type of curriculum will not be easy, and the reader will find further consideration of the issues raised in this chapter elsewhere in the book. It requires the teacher to have a wider and deeper knowledge of social processes than is customary at present; it requires much of the pupil; and it will provoke considerable reaction from the establishment. Nevertheless to me it seems imperative that geographers attempt to deal with some of the issues raised here. The alternative is for the subject to wither in its refusal to face the deep and real issues of modern society.

References

1 D. Stoddart, 'Kropotkin, Reclus and "relevant" geography', *Area*, 7 (1975), p. 188.
2 Ibid, p. 189.
3 W. Bunge, 'The Canadian-American Geographical Expedition', *Union of Socialist Geographers Newsletter*, 3, 1 (1977), p. 14.
4 R. Peet (ed.), *Radical Geography* (Methuen, 1977).
5 R. Peet, 'The development of radical geography in the United States', *Progress in Human Geography*, 1, 2 (1977), p. 244.
6 Membership details are available from the author, Department of Social Studies, Walton House, Liverpool Polytechnic, Liverpool L2 2NG.
7 Quoted in R. J. Johnson, *Geography and Geographers: Anglo-American Human Geography since 1945* (Edward Arnold, 1979), p. 172.
8 Since this chapter was written Dawn Gill has provided a further radical critique of the Avery Hill 14–16 Project in *Bulletin of Environmental Education*, 124 (Aug/Sept 1981) to which Rex Beddis has replied in *BEE*, 126 (Nov 1981).

Further reading

R. J. Johnston, *City and Society: an Outline for Urban Geography* (Penguin, 1980).
J. Harrison, *Marxist Economics for Socialists: a Critique of Reformism* (Pluto Press, 1978).
P. Harrison, *The Third World Tomorrow* (Penguin, 1980).
M. Quaini, *Geography and Marxism* (Blackwell, 1982).
G. Woodcock, *Anarchism* (Penguin, 1975).

Chapter 8

Political education

John Huckle

Having been reminded by academics that both landscapes and curricula are in part the products of political forces, geography teachers should adopt a considered approach to their inevitable role as agents of political education. This brief chapter reviews the main approaches to politics in schools, and suggests that there is much scope for cultivating political literacy within the geography curriculum. It outlines a framework for such literacy, and suggests how it may be applied in teaching about environmental planning and such related issues as nuclear power.

In any society disputes arise over social objectives and the means whereby these may be attained with limited resources. Politics deals with such disputes, and many of its central problems are concerned with resource distribution; with 'who gets what, where, and how'. The late 1970s saw a re-emergence of political geography,[1] as many academics focused their attention on the spatial and environmental consequences of diverse political policies, and sought to relate uneven resource distributions to underlying political power structures, processes, and theories. Such structural approaches are now applied to a wide range of phenomena at a variety of scales, and are particularly influential in the fields of economic, urban, and social geography.

The social climate which prompted geographers to seek greater social relevance and political awareness also revived the perennial debate on political education in schools. While some social scientists argued that economics, sociology, and politics deserved greater attention in the curriculum, others were exposing the strong legacy of indoctrination or social adjustment inherent in much teaching about society. Politics had either been ignored, or handled in such a way as to emphasize consensus and serve as 'instruction in obedience'.[2] The result was politically ignorant young adults whose general apathy and alienation threatened the future of democracy. Increasing economic and political tensions served to highlight their condition as the young unemployed became the ready recruits of extremist organizations, and adolescents expressed their nihilism in new cultural forms.

One result of increased awareness of political ignorance and apathy amongst school leavers was the Programme for Political Education established by the Hansard Society in 1974. This recommended a basic provision of political education in the common curriculum of all secondary schools, and established guidelines for teachers by 1978.[3] These suggest how all pupils can attain a basic level of political competence or literacy, by being taught to employ political concepts to analyse issues in ways which avoid bias and indoctrination, and respect reason and autonomy.

The working papers on the core curriculum which the Department of

Education and Science issued in 1977,[4] recognized the 'social and political' as one of eight areas of experience which schools should cultivate. A supplementary paper on political competence[5] clearly acknowledged the concept of political literacy, but much of the subsequent advocacy of political education was linked to the notion of 'the virtuous citizen' who had 'appropriate attitudes to the world of work'.[6] The tensions between those seeking genuine autonomy based on realistic attitudes to social conflict and those who could be seen to be employing political education as a form of political socialization in troubled times grew more acute after the Conservative government came to power in 1979.

Alternative approaches in schools

In the early 1980s there are renewed pressures to employ the curriculum as a means of adjusting pupils' aspirations to 'realistic' levels, and instilling 'responsible' attitudes. The geography curriculum has been guilty of fostering an uncritical respect for social values and institutions in the past, and teachers will need constantly to evaluate their approach if they are to minimize such indoctrination in the future.

In the majority of schools at present any political education that occurs is an incidental and unplanned outcome of both the hidden curriculum and the study of such subjects as history and geography. This incidental approach not only leads to indoctrination, but fails to develop the pupil's ability to think and act politically, in a logical and coherent way. It leaves too much to chance, and enables teachers to overlook their shared responsibility for developing political competence. The situation is little improved in schools which seek to teach the basic information of politics via a factual outline of key institutions and processes. Without the conceptual and practical skills to retain, organize, and use this knowledge, pupils are unlikely to develop genuine political understanding and the desire and ability to participate in a democracy. Many case studies, games, and decision-making exercises now take the geography teacher beyond mere political information,[7] and offer a real contribution to political literacy. Other lessons, however, ignore politics, contain elements of indoctrination, or merely transmit information, often in a boring way.

Political literacy

'A politically literate person will then know what the main political
disputes are about; what beliefs the main contestants have of them;
how they are likely to affect him, and he will have a predisposition to
try to do something about it in a manner at once effective and
respectful of the sincerity of others.'[8]

The approach advocated by the Programme for Political Education is based on the belief that political literacy can be developed by direct teaching of appropriate knowledge, skills, and attitudes. Its framework for such literacy

Knowledge		Skills		Attitudes and procedural values
Propositional knowledge	*Practical knowledge and understanding*	*Intellectual skills* / *Action skills*	*Communication skills*	

Within given political contexts (e.g. the state, workplace, union, college, school, etc.) the politically literate individual should know something about:

1 the structure of power;
2 customary ways of taking decisions and settling disputes;
3 alternative ways and means of taking decisions and settling disputes;
4 where the resources (money, goods, time, space, etc.) come from and how they are allocated;
5 alternative ways of allocating resources;
6 the main political issues and disputes;
7 who promotes what policies, goals or values, and why.

Practical knowledge and understanding

1 Some understanding of the nature of political disputes and issues (whether they are about goals, values, methods or results) and their causes.
2 Some understanding of how these political disputes might affect oneself and the groups to which one belongs.
3 Some understanding of how these disputes affect other people and the groups to which they belong.
4 Knowledge of how to influence the decision-making process in given contexts, including knowledge of alternative means of influence and their relative appropriateness for particular purposes.
5 A developing understanding of basic political concepts (conflict, decision-making, power, consent-dissent, order-disorder, and rules).
6 Knowledge of how to obtain information which one lacks.

Intellectual skills

1 Ability to interpret and evaluate political information and evidence.
2 Ability to organize information through basic political concepts and generalizations
3 Ability to apply reasoning skills to political problems and construct sound arguments based on evidence.
4 Ability to perceive the consequences of taking or not taking specific political actions in given contexts.

Action skills

1 Ability to participate in group decision-making.
2 Ability to effectively influence and/or change political situations.

Communication skills

1 Ability to express one's own interests, beliefs and viewpoints through an appropriate medium (oral or written).
2 Ability to participate in political discussion and debate.
3 Ability to perceive and understand (if not agree with) the interests, beliefs and views of others.
4 Ability to exercise empathy (i.e. to imagine what it might be like in someone else's shoes).

Attitudes and procedural values

1 Willingness to adopt a critical stance toward political information.
2 Willingness to give reasons why one holds a view or acts in a certain way and to expect similar reasons from others.
3 Respect for evidence in forming and holding political opinions.
4 Willingness to be open to the possibility of changing one's own attitudes and values in the light of evidence.
5 Value fairness as a criterion for judging and making decisions (i.e. regardless of whether the outcome will personally benefit or harm oneself).
6 Value the freedom to choose between political alternatives (goals, methods, values, parties or groups).
7 Toleration of a diversity of ideas, beliefs, values and interests.

Fig. 13   A framework for political literacy (source: Stradling, ref. 9)

(Figure 13)[9] is an attempt both to outline these components and to provide teachers with a checklist to aid course design. The knowledge enables pupils to understand the political dimensions of situations which affect their everyday lives, while the skills facilitate political expression and participation in strategies for change. Attitudes and procedural values encourage a commitment to rationality and tolerance, and a readiness to recognize and accept the inevitability of real political conflict in everyday life. Of prime importance in the framework are such basic political concepts as power, justice, and welfare, which help pupils to organize information and generalize to new situations.

In addition to its curriculum framework the Programme for Political Education provides guidelines for handling controversial issues in the classroom. Issues reflecting the politics of everyday life are considered the best vehicles for developing political literacy, and the teacher is advised to handle these through structured discussion which respects procedural values. By focusing on the following questions,[10] pupils would apply concepts, debate possible political solutions, and clarify their own positions:

i) In what form is the dispute expressed?
ii) What are the sources of the dispute?
iii) What is the nature of the issue?
iv) Who are involved in the dispute and which standpoints do they adopt?
v) What opportunities are open to them to influence the outcome of the dispute?
vi) What methods of influence do they or can they use?

Political action and participation

A further approach to political education stresses activism and community involvement. Its supporters[11] suggest that politics is learnt by doing, and that social action and participation are often more effective means of education than instilling knowledge and thinking skills. The more radical amongst them maintain that only by continually applying and revising knowledge in the real world will teachers and pupils attain a critical consciousness which is continually able to unmask ideology and perceive the real causes of social injustice. Since politics is omnipresent in social situations, they advocate participation in institutional and community issues as the best introduction to conflicting interests and power, and the various means of realizing considered goals. While such teachers as Chris Webb (Chapter 11) have successfully implemented this approach, others question its relevance in conventional educational settings. Their claims that schools allow limited scope for activism, and that practical politics quickly leads to controversy, are partly refuted by the experiences of teachers and pupils who have carried out community projects of the type suggested by such agencies as Community Service Volunteers.[12] The reflection prompted by such activity can be a great boost to the attainment of political literacy.

A Propositional knowledge of:
— those political contexts within which decisions affecting the environment take place,
   e.g. local naturalist trust, borough planning department, state, multinational corporation, United Nations Environment Programme.
— the structure and origins of power within such contexts,
   e.g. support and finance for road haulage lobby and anti-motorway campaigners.
— the different ways and means of taking decisions, allocating resources, and settling disputes,
   e.g. public participation in energy policy decisions in Britain, Sweden, West Germany, and Austria.
— the main issues in environmental politics and the social groups promoting different policies, goals, and values,
   e.g. policies of major political parties, trade unions, and pressure groups on such issues as recycling, energy conservation, appropriate technology, and job creation.

B Practical knowledge of:
— the nature of political disputes over environmental issues and their likely causes,
   e.g. an understanding of the differing meanings and political interpretations given to the term 'conservation'.
— how environmental issues affect oneself and others,
   e.g. the personal and social implications of different levels of intensification in agriculture.
— how to influence environmental decision-making by conventional or alternative means,
   e.g. case study of local campaign for air pollution control at nearby factory.
— alternative sources of environmental information,
   e.g. library study to reveal differing proposed optimum exploitation rates for North Sea oil.
— basic political concepts central to environmental politics,
   e.g. the meanings of welfare reflected in the various attitudes of employers and trade unions towards the nature of the work environment.

C Skills
The development of the intellectual, communication, and action skills, listed in Figure 13, is dependent on the teacher providing real or simulated experience of environmental decision-making and action.

D Attitudes and procedural values (as in Figure 13).

Fig. 14   Components of political literacy in the field of environmental management and planning

Environmental issues—nuclear power

Environmental management and planning are areas in which geography can make a major contribution to political literacy. Figure 14 lists the knowledge and skills which would appear to be relevant, and gives examples of curriculum topics in which they might be introduced. These should cover a wide range of political systems and ideologies at a variety of scales, and should suggest to pupils that differing theories about people and environments can serve differing political ends. Such concepts as justice and welfare can take on widely different meanings within the field of environmental politics, a fact which we are often too ready to overlook (Chapter 10). The need for greater political awareness in handling environmental issues is well illustrated by the topic of nuclear power.

'Do you think it is correct to call nuclear energy the power of the future?

Give reasons for your answer.'[13] In geography lessons the issue of nuclear power is too frequently presented as a technical option to be decided by weighing up such costs and benefits as reactor accidents, health risks, waste disposal, and 'cheap and reliable' electricity. The nuclear industry is currently providing teachers with impressive literature and expert speakers to foster such debate, while the anti-nuclear lobby has available alternative information. The technical and economic arguments are clearly open to interpretation, but the main function of much debate in both classrooms and the wider world is to conceal the political dimensions of the nuclear option and its hidden social agenda.[14] The acceptance of nuclear power is thought by some to lead to a more centralized and less democratic society.

In order to contribute to pupils' political literacy, a study of nuclear energy should look beyond the supposed costs and benefits to reveal the interests involved. The nuclear lobby is a powerful force within the corporate state, comprising government, the Central Electricity Generating Board, the Atomic Energy Authority, and large multinational companies with interests in energy and engineering. Since the 1950s it has conditioned the public to expect 'cheap' plentiful electricity, and even in the face of an energy crisis, sustains an expensive public relations programme designed to convince us that 'electricity is clean simplicity'. Anti-nuclear groups have limited resources to challenge such claims with alternative scientific evidence and energy policies, but they do emphasize the widely differing social implications of high and appropriate energy technology for the future of employment and civil liberties. Nuclear power would further centralize control over investment and production, would keep decisions in the hands of experts, and would maintain passive consumerism. The implementation of alternative energy policies, reflecting the needs of people rather than capital, could allow greater equality, sense of community, and public participation to develop.

Exposure to the literature and argument of a wide range of interest groups may gradually convince pupils that the nuclear debate is central to a consideration of how we wish to live in the future. The teacher should then ask them to assess the probable impacts of a nuclear economy in the light of their chosen values. Their conclusions will provide evidence of varying levels of political literacy, but this could simply lead to frustration or apathy if pupils are not shown how to make their influence felt in the real world. An examination of the policies and activities of political parties, trade unions, and pressure groups would aid pupils' perception of opportunities to exert political influence, and would provide a foundation for future participation within the democratic political process. Those who argue that students of fifteen and sixteen are not ready to grapple with such issues should remember that in two or three years those students will be voting for politicians who are often only too ready to justify energy policy in terms of technical necessity.

The challenge of political education

While geographers were not involved in the work of the Programme for Political Education, reforms in political geography and a shift to more open and critical classrooms place us in a strong position to take up the challenge presented by political education. If we are to introduce older pupils to the political explanations offered by welfare and radical geographers, while at the same time seeking opportunities for real community participation, we will need the defences which the theory and practice of political education can now provide. In enabling committed teachers to consider rationally the causes of mounting unemployment, a nuclear economy, racism and a deteriorating welfare state, political education offers at least some prospect of countering the growing apathy and alienation which now threaten us all.

References

1   See the reviews of recent developments in political geography by P. J. Taylor in *Progress in Human Geography*, 2 (1978) and 3 (1979), and by S. Clark Archer in the same journal, 4 (1980).

2   J. Beck, 'Social and political education: a question of priorities', *Cambridge Journal of Education*, 8, 2 and 3 (1978).

3   B. Crick and A. Porter (eds.), *Political Education and Political Literacy* (Longman, 1978).

4   *Curriculum 11-16*, Working papers by HM Inspectorate (DES/HMSO, 1977).

5   'Now is the time for all good men to stop being coy about political education', *Times Educational Supplement*, 25/11/77.

6   J. Beck, op. cit. (ref. 2).

7   T. Gelsthorpe, 'The contribution of geography to political education', *Teaching Politics*, 6 (1977).

8   B. Crick and I. Lister, *A Programme for Political Education—an explanatory paper* (Hansard Society, 1974).

9   R. Stradling, 'Political education in the 11–16 curriculum', *Cambridge Journal of Education*, 8, 2 and 3 (1978).

10   R. Stradling and A. Porter, *Issues and Political Problems* (Hansard Society, 1976).

11   H. Entwhistle, 'Education and the concept of political socialization', *Teaching Politics*, 3, 2 (1974).

12   A. Griffith and C. Moffat, *The School in Action* (Community Service Volunteers, 1977) and M. Norton, *Planning your Environment* (Community Service Volunteers, 1976).

13   N. Graves and J. White, *Geography of the British Isles* (Heinemann, 1971), p. 166.

14   S. Croall and K. Sempler, *Nuclear Power for Beginners* (Beginners Books, 1978).
      D. Elliot *et al.*, *The Politics of Nuclear Power* (Pluto Press, 1978).

Chapter 9

Development education

David Hicks

Issues of development and underdevelopment, minority rights, race and racism are of vital concern today. They impinge, directly or indirectly, on life both in and outside the classroom. They are issues which should be studied in geography at a variety of scales from the local to the global. Traditionally, geographers have either avoided these issues or treated them superficially. They have been taken up, however, by the two overlapping fields of development education and multi-ethnic education. This chapter thus sets out to clarify the main features and tensions within these two areas of concern and their relevance to a committed geography.

Development education had its origins in the late 1960s, when international organizations and voluntary agencies concerned with global inequalities felt that education about issues of development was needed in the rich nations of the North. During the 1970s, however, it became apparent that the term was being used in a variety of different ways. Broadly speaking, people's understanding of development education can be placed on a spectrum, at the traditional or closed end of which it is seen as teaching about Third World problems. This is still probably the most common type of development education. Somewhere in the middle of the spectrum it is seen as being about North-South relationships, with the focus more on interdependence and a global perspective. Problems are thus seen as global rather than occurring only in the Third World. Solutions, however, are still often seen as 'more of before', e.g. technology, aid or food. In the classroom the concern is with changing students' attitudes as well as transmitting the facts.

At the open end of the spectrum development education is seen as having global, national, local, and even personal dimensions and as being very much about changing eurocentric viewpoints. It argues the need for structural change, not only in the so-called Third World, but in particular in the global power-holding nations of the rich North. The links are clearly drawn, past and present, between our lives and the exploitation of Third World peoples today. It is this open end of the spectrum which concerns us, for only here is a fundamental analysis of the issues attempted. Perhaps the best definition is that of the United Nations:

> 'The objective of development education is to enable people to participate in the development of their community, their nation, and the world as a whole. Such participation implies a critical awareness of local, national and international situations based on an understanding of the social, economic, and political processes.
>
> Development education is concerned with issues of human rights, dignity, self-reliance, and social justice in both developed and

developing countries. It is concerned with the causes of under-development and a promotion of an understanding of what is involved in development, of how different countries go about undertaking development, and of the reasons for and ways of achieving a new international economic and social order.'

In several European countries funds for development education are allocated from the official aid budget. In 1975 Sweden, Norway, and the Netherlands each spent 0.5 per cent of their official aid in this way, whilst Britain spent 0.03 per cent. Thus in 1977, under the Labour Government, the Ministry for Overseas Development set up an Advisory Committee on Development Education which in turn recommended spending £2 million per annum on development education. This fund enabled many useful projects to start up but it was cut by the Conservative Government, which also downgraded the Ministry to the Overseas Development Administration.

Many of the best development education materials are available from the specialist education departments of voluntary agencies such as Oxfam and Christian Aid. It is important at this point also to recall that development education is only one of a range of overlapping concerns focusing on contemporary global issues. These include: world studies, peace studies, and education for international understanding, all of which have been very usefully described by Derek Heater.[1]

Colonialism and racism

British images of continents such as Africa and Asia can be understood only in the light of Britain's relationships to such areas over the last 200 years or so. Britain's role was, of course, that of a colonizing imperial power, and it was only in 1933 that the British Empire reached its geographical maximum as the largest area of conquered territory in world history.

Colonial attitudes to the subjects of Empire, Kipling's 'lesser breeds without the law', crystallized in the late nineteenth century as ideas about race and pride in Empire began to fuse. Thus, quite simply, Europeans measured other cultures against their own norms (this is ethnocentrism) and obviously found them lacking; by all the 'correct' indices others were uncivilized. Since the Victorians saw the world as a very hierarchical place they classified other peoples by race. Clearly the British were at the top whilst other races were inferior. Labelling other peoples as inferior, or seeing oneself as superior, whether due to alleged biological, cultural, or social differences is, simply, to be racist. Historically therefore Britain has viewed the Third World in both an ethnocentric and racist way. Racist assumptions today are thus not the result of personality defect but, rather, part of our cultural heritage and childhood socialization. Indeed a recent attitude survey described the British as suffering from 'national introversion' and many of the attitudes expressed about overseas aid were straight from the heyday of Empire.

As teachers we should expect students to be ethnocentric and racist, indeed as John Carnie[2] has shown they form their attitudes to other nationalities at a very early age. Having been made aware of this it is our duty to explore non-racist and anti-racist ways of teaching, a theme taken up again at the end of this chapter.

Development and underdevelopment

Given the above we should not be surprised that traditional views about development and underdevelopment are biased against poor people. Underdevelopment is thus often considered to be a state which Third World countries merely happen to find themselves in. The assumed reasons for this range from environmental hazards and overpopulation to inefficient farming and political mismanagement. The causes of underdevelopment are thus identified as internal, inherent obstacles. Countries need to escape from this and achieve a developed state by programmes of modernization and economic growth. Benefits are supposed to accrue to the population at large by a trickle-down effect. Development is thus seen as linear with take-off occurring from one type of impoverished society to the preferred European/American dream.

Alternative views of development and underdevelopment have gained considerable ground in the 1970s both in the North and South. On this basis underdevelopment is best seen, not as a state, but rather as a process arising out of the unequal relationship between colonized and colonizer. Colonialism often disrupted indigenous social systems and replaced them with an inappropriate veneer of westernization; local industries were crippled to promote British exports and subsistence farming often replaced by a plantation economy. The Third World became a mere supplier of raw materials to the North, an image which some textbooks still convey.

Neo-colonial patterns of dependency are, of course, still the norm since the North controls world trade, research and technology, commodity prices, aid, the media, and the arms trade. To suggest that Britain was one of the countries that helped to create underdevelopment and that, as one of the rich countries of the world, we continue to promote it is an uncomfortable thought. An ethnocentric perspective leads to the rejection of such perspectives.

Paul Harrison[3] has graphically described the new concepts of development such as self-help co-operatives, small-scale appropriate technologies and a stress on basic needs, all of which start not with grand economic programmes but with the needs of the most oppressed groups as expressed by themselves. Development is thus best seen as being about the development of human beings rather than of countries or the production of things. Russell King has also succinctly summarized some of the main issues.[4]

Teaching about world development

So what does development education have to offer geography teaching? At its best there are many points where it relates to a committed geography curriculum. Over the last decade geography teachers have increasingly come to see the Third World as an important area for study. The danger, of course, is that the Third World (a term taken by some to imply inferiority) with its problems becomes the sole focus of attention. This is a danger that geographers must avoid, for rather than focusing on Third World problems we should be looking at the nature of North–South relationships and their inbuilt inequality.

What themes might we therefore deal with in the classroom? A geography study group drew up this useful checklist[5] to apply to textbooks, but it can equally be applied to the curriculum. Does the curriculum:

1 deal with spatial variations in the levels of human welfare, measured on a variety of scales? Does it consider the validity of measures of human welfare, e.g. GNP?
2 indicate ethnic and cultural diversity and the plural nature of many societies?
3 show any awareness of the cultural achievements of developing countries and the cultural debts that industrialized countries owe to them?
4 discuss the physical environment in terms of constraints upon, and opportunities for, development?
5 deal with the history of the developing countries concerned, with reference to their colonial background?
6 deal with the world distribution of resources and production?
7 deal with the content and direction of international trade, its changing patterns and the ways in which it affects the internal structure of developing countries?
8 discuss occupational structures and the kinds of work that people do?
9 present a range of agricultural situations in developing countries and discuss questions of land ownership and land reform?
10 deal with population increase rates, age structures, and densities? Does it explain the causes of change?
11 look at migration flows within developing countries (e.g. urbanization) and at international migration, past and present?
12 discuss different types of human settlements and their characteristics and functions ?
13 discuss the nature of aid relationships?
14 look at alternative strategies for development?
15 examine the economic, social, and cultural effects of tourism?
16 include any discussion of the role of large multinational corporations?

David Wright[6] also pointed the way ahead when he suggested the need for an 'idea-swap' on questions such as:

Does appropriate technology get enough attention?
Why are plantations treated as value-free case studies? They raise lots of ethical and political questions.
Marxist approaches to development can no longer be ignored: lots of Third World countries now follow Marxist ideas. How best can we teach about them?
Are our areas for study far too hackneyed? For example, why are francophone Africa and Turkey hardly ever studied? Turkey is a fascinating example

of deliberate westernization, and francophone Africa is half a continent.
Do we give enough attention to Third World cities, and what approaches to such study work best?
Is an emphasis on problems counter-productive in terms of attitude formation?
How are new themes best introduced, for example the new economic order and the basic needs approach to development?

A final point needs to be made here about textbooks, which are still very important in upper school work. A detailed survey of twenty popular text-books and their assumptions, explicit and implicit, about the Third World showed that overall they contained six clear messages: (i) the main problem today is the Third World; (ii) Third World poverty is due to a combination of chance and inbuilt obstacles; (iii) follow the example of the North and take-off to development will occur; (iv) there are too many hungry people in the Third World; (v) peasant farmers need educating and everyone needs help; (vi) colonialism is nothing to do with geography.[7]

Given what has been said previously we should not find this surprising. Taking books individually some are clearly less biased than others. Although all are variable in quality, amongst the more useful would be Clare's *The Third World* (Macdonald), Simons's *Poverty and Wealth in Cities and Villages* (OUP), Reed's *The Developing World* (Bell & Hyman), and Young and Lowry's, Book 10, *The World: A Systematic Geography* (Arnold). To be avoided, or better still analysed by the students themselves for racist bias, would be Davies's *Problems Around Us* (Holmes McDougall) and Ferris and Toyne's *World Problems* (Hulton).

We need to submit ourselves as committed geographers to a continuous process of re-education on these issues. The information is there if we look for it. No one should teach about world food, for example, before reading Susan George's *How the Other Half Dies: The Real Reasons for World Hunger* (Pelican) or Lappé and Collins's *Food First: Beyond the Myth of Scarcity* (Souvenir Press).

Geography in a multi-ethnic curriculum

Britain, having underdeveloped its colonies, and with the age of colonialism past, looked to its former territories to supplement its own workforce in the 1950s and 1960s. This set the stage for a new conflict between the colonial and indigenous workforces which was accentuated by the fact that the confrontation took place in marginal areas of employment. Many race relations problems are better seen as colonial problems and the arrival of formerly conquered subjects only highlighted the decline of the British Empire and its 'glories'. The shortage of labour at the time made immigrants economically acceptable. In periods of full employment indigenous workers moved upwards leaving the worst work to immigrant labour in already existing underprivileged situations.

Given the extent of racism in Britain it is not surprising that surveys of public attitudes find a close correlation between attitudes to the Third World and ethnic minority groups in Britain. The widespread nature of discrimination has been documented by Smith in his *Racial Disadvantages in Britain* (Pelican). It is the extent of this discrimination and what it feels like to suffer it continuously that teachers need to understand. One of the best introductions to children and race has been written by Rosalind Street-Porter[8] and clearly sets out the main issues. It is against this overall context that multi-ethnic education must be seen.

The school curriculum tends to be ethnocentric because it mirrors society at large; that is, it ignores the perspectives and needs of Third World peoples and minority groups within the UK. Any curriculum that is to reflect the priorities of our plural society should (i) be aware of the nature of children's racial attitudes and the need to combat prejudice, and (ii) meet the needs of children from different minority groups, whether related to poor self-image or underachievement in the classroom. These factors are often very much part of the minority experience, in no way inherent, but a response to continuous majority prejudice.

Various terms are used to describe a curriculum which attempts to be less ethnocentric, e.g. multiracial, multicultural, and multi-ethnic. Multiracial is less in favour now as it could be taken to imply the existence of discrete 'races' which, in fact, do not exist. Multicultural is used more often although, again, many minority group members may possess no distinct culture of their own (e.g. black British students). Multi-ethnic is increasingly used to denote concern for all groups within a society. The arguments about terminology tend to be confused and will probably remain so.

So what does a multi-ethnic curriculum look like? The traditional time-table tends to be ethnocentric as does the occasional project on India or the Caribbean. A multi-ethnic curriculum may indeed include the latter, but it must also be much more. Whether for schools in all white areas (where it is equally important) or in areas with minority group children, a multi-ethnic curriculum should influence the whole ethos of the school. It involves continuous recognition of the multi-ethnic nature of society locally, nationally, and globally. All schools should ask the following questions about the curriculum: does it consider the diverse contributions made to society by other cultures past and present? does it acknowledge that children are aware of racial differences and similarities at an early age and that they need to discuss these? does it discuss ideas about race and the history of migration? is the presence of the racial prejudice in society accepted, explained fully, or opposed?

In a multi-ethnic classroom one also needs to consider: the dangers of the colour-blind approach which imagines all children are exactly the same; the self-fulfilling nature of low pupil expectation; the importance of children's mother-tongue needs; the need for encouraging self-respect and cultural identity in a plural society.

Whilst all these issues often need direct and skilful handling in the classroom, it is often useful to use a distancing effect by looking at majority/minority issues in other parts of the world first. This may help to avoid the interference often caused by strong emotional reactions arising out of racism in the local community. One example of this approach, of interest to geographers, includes case studies of Sahel nomads, native Americans, and the struggle for Aborigines' land-rights.[9]

Links between development and multi-ethnic education

It is important to note here that there need be no clash between the perspectives of development education and multi-ethnic education. Just as definitions of development education can be placed on an open-closed spectrum, so can responses to multi-ethnic education. Thus at the closed end of such a spectrum the focus is on the problems caused by immigrants and the need for them to assimilate into white society. Towards the middle of the spectrum the focus is on race relations and getting on well together, the keynotes being tolerance and attitude change. At the open end of the spectrum (which is the one that concerns us here) the emphasis is on respect for self and others, building a positive self-image, cultural and ethnic autonomy, and the structural change required for a more just society.

It is at the open end of both spectrums that multi-ethnic education and development education can be seen to be two sides of the same coin, united in a concern for social justice.[10] At the closed end of each spectrum they have nothing in common and are extremely ethnocentric, i.e. development education is about the problems of Third World poverty and multi-ethnic education is about teaching English to immigrants (who may in fact have been born here). Such definitions and expectations need to be constantly challenged.

Geography and development education

In a recent survey three-quarters of a sample of geography teachers felt that geography ought to teach about the plural nature of British society. However, if we look at commonly used textbooks on the British Isles, there are in fact very few references to minority groups. They are generally limited to a paragraph or, more often, only a few lines. As yet geography textbooks contribute little to multi-ethnic understanding. The two books which are in the lead here are Turner's *Spotlight on the UK* (Macmillan) and Marsden's *The Changing Geography of Britain* (Oliver & Boyd), both to be recommended.

If we acknowledge that race is a social classification and not a biological one,[11] what should the contribution of geography be here? As far as the geography of the British Isles is concerned the plural nature of society is a basic factor in many patterns, e.g. residential patterns, employment patterns, population composition, city zoning, migration of people, the growth of ports based on the slave-trade revenue. To this one could add as focal points for study the quality of the environment, human welfare, and social justice. These must not be taken, however, as a mere shopping list of topics, for it is the processes that create the patterns that need to be highlighted. A committed geography does not accept society as it is—an unjust status quo—but works to change it.

Good development education is also very much part of multi-ethnic geography because attitudes towards ethnic minority groups in the UK are, in part, influenced by the images of their assumed Third World homelands. Thus the exotic, problem, or overemphasized poverty images must be avoided. Global themes on inequality, population, migration, and urbanism are all important, as also may be case studies on the Caribbean, India, and South Africa. Neither should the historical dimension be ignored, for many of today's patterns can only be understood in the light of colonial decision-making. When studying majority/minority issues elsewhere in the world the social, political, and economic contexts must not be forgotten. For example, not only climatic figures for tea-growing, but also living conditions on tea plantations and the nature of the Tamil/Sinhalese clash must be considered; not only methods of gold mining, but also the migrant labour system, and the nature and injustice of apartheid; not only the methods of shifting cultivation, but also the sophisticated ecological awareness of so-called primitive peoples.

So where do we start in the classroom? Geographers have been slow, so far, to produce their own unbiased resources on these themes. Very useful materials are available, however, and, although they are only a beginning, they offer several exciting starting-points for teachers and students. Addresses of organizations are given at the end of this chapter. These books, packs, and films are not universal panaceas, they will only work after we have been through our own inner reflection and turmoil to face the racism and authoritarianism within ourselves.

One of the best resource books currently available is *Learning for Change in World Society* by Robin Richardson (World Studies Project) which is an excellent compendium of activities for classroom use. They provide opportunities 'for students not only to learn about the wider world but also about themselves, their friends and their relationships, their immediate situation.' The activities are seen as tools to transform problems (e.g. controversy, identity in a group, authority in the classroom) into resources. *The Development Puzzle* (Centre for World Development Education) is also a sourcebook for teachers on the rich world/poor world divide and global development. It is full of teaching ideas and has an exhaustive resources section.

Ideas into Action (World Studies Project) is a handbook for teachers, written by teachers, and contains thirteen case studies which develop global and multi-ethnic perspectives in school, either through courses or projects or across the curriculum. If you want good films and ideas on how to use them, consult *Seeing and Perceiving: Films in a World of Change* (Concord Films Council), a perceptive and useful analysis of how to use films to maximum effect in the classroom with details of some of the best ones available. *Divide and Rule—Never!* (Newsreel Collective) is a stimulating collection of support materials to go with the film of the same name, made to promote discussion and action on racism in Britain today.

Two periodicals that all staffrooms should take are *New Approaches in Multiracial Education* (National Association for Multiracial Education) and the

World Studies Journal (Groby Community College), each with a good balance of theoretical and practical articles. *Natural Peoples News* (Colonial and Indigenous Minorities Research Association) is a regular compendium of newspaper cuttings on minority issues around the world, often dealing with the role of giant multinational mining corporations in underdevelopment, whilst *From Massacres to Mining* (War on Want) deals graphically with the colonization and exploitation of Aboriginal Australia up to the present day.

Two useful packs for older students are *Change and Choice: Britain in an Interdependent World* which shows the links between the local and global village, and *Choices in Development* which examines the different models of development used in Kenya and Tanzania (both from the Centre for World Development Education). Useful textbooks are Wright's *West Indies* (Longman), Stuart's *Unequal Third* (Arnold), Turner's *World Inequality* (Longman), and Richardson's *World Studies* series (Nelson). Excellent materials on the black British experience are available (ACER Project) and Searle's *The World in a Classroom* (Writers and Readers Publishing Co-operative) illustrates the sort of writing that students can produce on all these contemporary themes.

Controversy, conflicting value-positions, social change, human welfare, these are the exciting and dynamic issues into which a committed geography leads us and to which critical development education and multi-ethnic education can contribute. As Brian Wren[12] has shown, 'education for justice' begins in our own classrooms with the relationships that we build there. It continues when we face our own ethnocentrism and racism and really begin to listen to the voices of Third World peoples and minority groups. From that listening, and the reflection and understanding that follow, can come action and commitment to an anti-racist stance, for what passes as neutrality is not objectivity but assent to an unjust status quo.

References

1   D. Heater, *World Studies: Education for International Understanding in Britain* (Harrap, 1980).
2   J. Carnie, 'Children's attitudes to other nationalities', *New Movements in the Study and Teaching of Geography* (Temple Smith, 1972), Chapter 10.
3   P. Harrison, *The Third World Tomorrow* (Penguin, 1980).
4   R. King, 'Alternative approaches to the geography of development', *Teaching Geography*, 2, 2 (1976).
5   *The Changing World and Geography* (Centre for World Development Education, 1979).
6   D. Wright, 'Third World teaching: which way now?', *Times Educational Supplement*, Geography Extra, 10/11/78.
7   D. Hicks, *Images of the World: an Introduction to Bias in Teaching Materials,* Occasional Paper, and *Bias in Geography Textbooks: Images of the Third World and Multi-ethnic Britain,* Working Paper (Centre for Multicultural Education, University of London Institute of Education, 1980). Also 'The contribution of geography to multicultural misunderstanding', *Teaching Geography*, 7, 2 (1981).

8   R. Street-Porter, *Race, Children and Cities* (Open University Press, 1978), E361 Block V.
9   D. Hicks, *Minorities: A Teacher's Resource Book for the Multi-ethnic Curriculum* (Heinemann, 1981).
10 D. Hicks, 'Two sides of the same coin: an exploration of the links between multicultural education and development education', *New Approaches in Multiracial Education*, 7, 2 (1979).
11 *Race, Education, Intelligence* (National Union of Teachers, 1978).
12 B. Wren, *Education for Justice* (SCM Press, 1977).

Addresses

ACER Project (Afro-Caribbean Educational Resources), Centre for Learning Resources, 275 Kennington Lane, London SE11 5QZ.
Centre for World Development Education, 128 Buckingham Palace Road, London SW1V 1JS.
Colonial and Indigenous Minorities Research Association (CIMRA), 92 Plimsoll Road, London N4.
Concord Films Council, 201 Felixstowe Road, Ipswich, Suffolk IP3 9BJ.
Groby Community College, Ratby Road, Groby, Leicester LE6 0FP.
National Association for Multiracial Education (NAME), 23 Doles Lane, Findern, Derby DE6 6AX.
Newsreel Collective's film is available for hire from Concord Films Council (see above); the booklet can be requested when the film is hired.
War on Want, 467 Caledonian Road, London N7 9BE.
World Studies Project, 24 Palace Chambers, Bridge Street, London SW1A 2JT.

Chapter 10

Environmental education

John Huckle

> '. . . the ecology movement is not an end in itself but a stage
> in the larger struggle.'
> *André Gorz*

The modern ecology movement to which Gorz[1] refers began in the late 1960s
and attracted support from those concerned about the related issues of
environmental quality, resource depletion, and population growth on a
planet where more and more people were seeking a modern industrial
lifestyle. While support for the movement reached a peak in the mid 1970s,
and is now in decline, it has left a strong legacy in society and education
which no geography teacher can afford to ignore. This chapter therefore
explores the various ways in which environmentalists and teachers express
their concern for the environment and examines their significance for
geography in schools. It argues for a radical form of environmental education
supported by new insights from moral and political education.

The ecology movement was launched by certain ecologists, economists,
and others who forecast disaster unless the human population adjusted its
demands upon 'spaceship earth'. Updating Malthus with ideas from ecology,
they insisted that we were reaching the 'limits of growth' and that population
control and economic constraint were essential. Such early pessimism was
gradually modified as the movement shifted its attention to those psychological and social limits which we would need to overcome if a post-
industrial age were to dawn. Ecology became part of distinctive environmental philosophies which claimed to describe the transformations in human
ethics and society which were necessary to ensure our continued evolution
within nature. The current debate over the expansion of Britain's nuclear
power programme suggests that these philosophies continue to influence
political thought and action and to challenge the core values and institutions
of society.

Since the ecology movement attracts most of its support from the
relatively affluent middle class, it is not surprising that it appeals to many
teachers and has prompted them to seek interpretations of environmental
education which appear more relevant to perceived environmental issues.
This chapter suggests that such education takes three dominant forms in
Britain, each reflecting a distinctive set of environmental and educational
beliefs. Education *about* the environment and education *from* the environment
are the most widely established, but may be seen to sustain the general
deterioration in environmental quality. Only education *for* the environment
offers teachers the theory and practice with which to make a genuine

contribution to environmental well-being, and this requires an acknowledgement of the links between environmental, moral, and political education. By facilitating sound environmental decision-making and behaviour, in both personal and social contexts, geography teachers can begin to question prevailing values and reveal the true causes of environmental deterioration.

Environmental ideologies

Environmentalists are not united in either their analysis of our environmental predicament or their support for perceived solutions. Such concerns as population growth, pollution, nature conservation, architectural heritage, and radical technology appeal to a wide range of political persuasions, and prompt support for diverse policies at a variety of scales. The one thing that may be seen to characterize all environmentalists is their readiness to use a knowledge of environmental issues and ecology to gain support for particular social policies. Facts and theories about the environment are incorporated into coherent systems of beliefs which may serve as ideology by concealing the true nature of human-environment relations and maintaining the interests of particular social groups.[2] Environmental ideologies may offer diagnoses and prescriptions which appear to explain environmental problems and offer solutions, yet they are often a means of defusing public discontent and maintaining the existing form of economy and society. Teachers generally find expression for their environmental concerns within one or other of the available environmental ideologies and these are also reflected in curriculum materials. A commitment to educate for an improved environment necessitates an early examination of these ideologies.

i) Conventional environmentalism suggests that mounting environmental problems should prompt a greater attention to environmental management and planning which incorporates applied ecology. It maintains that ecological dangers can be avoided without major social and economic change, provided we incorporate ecology into existing decision-making frameworks. In outlining a typology of current environmental ideologies, Timothy O'Riordan[3] suggests that the technocentric supporters of the conventional viewpoint can be divided into cornucopians and accommodators (Figure 15). While cornucopians adopt a business-as-usual attitude and consider that talk of ecological limits is essentially scaremongering, accommodators or environmental managers are far more prepared to use economic, legislative, and technological means to reduce the environmental impacts of human activity. Both groups disregard major social transformations in the interest of the environment, but it is the accommodators who have perhaps had greatest influence on the science and geography curricula in schools. Techniques from such fields as welfare economics, systems analysis, and technology assessment have not failed to penetrate the classroom, and the rise of this ideology is not unrelated to increased pleas for co-operation between teachers and planners.

Environmentalism

Ecocentrism		Technocentrism	
Deep environmentalists	**Self-reliance soft technologists**	**Accommodators**	**Cornucopians**
3 Intrinsic importance of nature for the humanity of man	1 Lack of faith in modern large-scale technology and its associated demands on elitist expertise, central state authority and inherently anti-democratic institutions	1 Belief that economic growth and resource exploitation can continue assuming (a) suitable economic adjustments to taxes, fees, etc. (b) improvements in the legal rights to a minimum level of environmental quality (c) compensation arrangements satisfactory to those who experience adverse environmental and/or social effects	1 Belief that man can always find a way out of any difficulties either politically, scientifically or technologically
4 Ecological (and other natural) laws dictate human morality	2 Implication that materialism for its own sake is wrong and that economic growth can be geared to providing for the basic needs for those below subsistence levels	2 Acceptance of new project appraisal techniques and decision review arrangements to allow for wider discussion or genuine search for consensus among representative groups of interested parties	2 Acceptance that pro-growth goals define the rationality of a project appraisal and of policy formulation
5 Biorights—the right of endangered species or unique landscapes to remain unmolested	3 Emphasis on smallness of scale and hence community identity in settlement, work and leisure	3 Provision of effective environmental management agencies at national and local levels	3 Optimistic about the ability of man to improve the lot of the world's people
	4 Integration of concepts of work and leisure through a process of personal and communal improvement		4 Faith that scientific and technological expertise provides the basic foundation for advice on matters pertaining to economic growth, public health and safety
	5 Importance of participation in community affairs, and of guarantees of the rights of minority interests. Participation seen both as a continuing education and political function		5 Suspicious of attempts to widen basis for participation and lengthen discussion in project appraisal and policy review
			6 Belief that any impediments can be overcome given a will, ingenuity and sufficient resources arising out of wealth

Fig. 15 The pattern of environmental ideologies (source: O'Riordan, ref. 3)

ii) Utopian environmentalism exploits people's concern about the environment in order to gain support for utopian alternatives to prevailing conceptions of society. The deep environmentalists (Figure 15) believe that nature not only helps us understand ourselves and our world but is itself a source of moral values which impose limits on economic development. Drawing on transcendental philosophy and modern ecology, they propose new forms of natural morality and social organization at various scales from the local to the global and generally present these as ethical and apolitical necessities. Some continue to argue for steady-state economies and conservation strategies at the macro-level, while others attempt to implement blueprints for survival at the micro-level. Deep environmentalists are often prepared to impose frugal and authoritarian conditions on their fellow men and women, and pay little attention to the widening of inequalities which many of their proposals would entail.

A further group of utopians support some of the beliefs which O'Riordan attributes to the soft technologists. The surviving disciples of the student counter-culture of the late 1960s, they shun conventional society and advocate small-scale, self-reliant communities where it would be possible for people to enjoy liberated and creative lives in an open and permissive atmosphere. While deep environmentalists see ecological consciousness resulting from a return to more primitive and ordered forms of society, liberal utopians insist on the need for radically new forms of community based on freedom. Both groups are seen as politically naive, idealist, and retreatist by radical environmentalists.

iii) Radical environmentalism regards ecological problems as simply further evidence of the crises currently confronting industrial societies. Its followers regard disparities in environmental well-being as examples of more general disparities in social justice, and maintain that environmental abuse results from the normal operations of basic institutions in societies where economic needs generally dominate people's needs for high quality surroundings. Decisions taken by business executives, trans-national corporations, state bureaucrats, and others generally ensure that the environment is reduced to its instrumental role in sustaining the economy, and that genuine improvements in environmental quality can therefore result only from fundamental reforms of basic social and economic institutions. Radicals draw upon the ideas of Marxists, neo-Marxists, and anarchists, and, like conventionalists and utopians, disagree on the ideal route to reform.

Marxist elements amongst the radicals see a deteriorating environment as a symptom of the crises currently confronting advanced capitalism. By attempting to offset a crisis of capital overaccumulation by ever more wasteful and destructive production, economic decision-makers have brought about a situation in which the availability of previously cheap and plentiful resources, such as clean air or water, is ever more problematic. As industry adjusts to the new costs of creating such resources, the economy's overall efficiency falls and a spiral of inflation, recession, growing inequalities, and repression affects us all. Revolutionary change should focus on the transformation of the economy and decision-making in order to ensure production for genuine need rather than greed. For the majority of Marxists this means socialist planning and environmental management co-ordinated from above.

Another group of radicals, O'Riordan's soft technologists, are anxious to avoid the risks of oppression inherent in such calls for revolution. They are sympathetic to a Marxist account of the environmental crisis, but suggest that the rise of the corporate state and the power of organized labour have done much to weaken an orthodox diagnosis. Social and political action against alienated decision-making should, in their opinion, be focused at the base of society since a politically literate community is less likely to allow the drift to elitism, centralism, and corporatism which has followed so many socialist revolutions. Soft technologists seek the support of sympathetic experts, but do not share the illusions about the rationality and goodwill of those in power held by accommodators. They see their main task to be the politicization of environmental issues in order that the underprivileged recognize them to be intimately linked with such perennial concerns as housing, public transport, welfare, and unemployment. Only by raising consciousness in this way will radicals ensure that such issues as nuclear power gain the political scrutiny they deserve. Soft technologists or radical ecological activists claim to be open and critical compared with other environmentalists whose ideological blinkers frequently serve to sustain or worsen inequalities in environmental well-being. Like Gorz, they see the political struggle for the environment as 'but a stage in the larger struggle'.

From a radical viewpoint, conventional environmentalism appears to sustain the existing social order and its related inequalities since its beliefs and strategies largely ignore class relations and alternative patterns of economic organization. Environmental management and planning are essentially a means of preserving the existing mode of production and creating such new areas for capital investment as environmental protection. Capitalism is rarely prepared to put the environment before profit and readily transfers the costs of its environmental damage to workers and citizens.

Similarly, utopians are seen to pose no real threat to prevailing interests since they too divert attention away from the real causes of environmental abuse. Appeals for population control, nature conservation, and economic restraint enable capitalism to attribute its diminishing returns to nature or the poor, while the proposed utopias are feasible only for a small minority of people. Their idealism meets the socio-psychological needs of a disillusioned middle class whose environment is threatened for the first time in history, but is largely irrelevant to the vast majority which has far more pressing concerns.

The one clear and valid message of the ecology movement is that the natural environment does pose limits on economic development. While this fact has contributed to reactionary and idealistic ideas now revealed as ideology, it has also encouraged genuinely critical thought which has implications for education. It is to environmental education that we now turn.

Approaches to environmental education

Like the wider social movement which prompted its emergence, modern environmental education encompasses a wide range of disparate aims and interests. While its practitioners include those interested in local studies, urban education, environmental science, art, and human ecology, its major voice (the Council for Environmental Education) speaks for over fifty interested parties including Community Service Volunteers, the National Farmers' Union, the Royal Institute of British Architects, and the Independent Schools' Association. Environmental education has developed from roots in rural studies to embrace the urban environment, and has added to its objectives of imparting knowledge, skills and awareness, a concern for the pupils' attitudes and values as they affect environmental decision-making and behaviour. Official reports encourage teachers to regard environmental education as a responsibility across the curriculum with a wide range of outcomes, while summaries are available which outline current practice at both national and international levels.[4] These acknowledge varied activities in schools, but generally fail to relate them to the diverse environmental and educational beliefs via which they are justified. Distinct educational ideologies are commonly coupled with the environmental ideologies already described to give three contrasting forms of environmental studies in schools.

i) Education about the environment[5] reflects conventional environmentalism and liberal educational ideology. It views education and environmental management as neutral instruments of social policy, and suggests that by making the environment increasingly the *subject* of education schools can create an understanding of environmental issues and so contribute to sound environmental management. While curriculum content has a strongly scientific emphasis, stressing man's ability to plan and control his environment, teaching methods are generally formal and affective outcomes only acknowledged within decision-making exercises which reflect the pragmatism of the wider society. Curriculum integration, if it occurs, is a response to the perceived needs of future technocrats and has little influence on the social system of the school. This institution remains detached from the community and the immediate environment is either ignored or used solely as a teaching resource. Education *about* the environment forms a significant element of subject teaching in secondary schools and is exemplified by much of the new geography discussed in Chapter 14. It has attracted funding from private corporations and is well represented in many textbooks and examination syllabuses in everyday use.

ii) In seeking to use the environment as a *medium* for education, **education from the environment** reflects the idealism which underlies both utopian environmentalism and progressive education. In the tradition of Rousseau and others, it employs environmental studies as a rationale for pupil-centred, topic-based learning which often reflects a rather naive respect for both children and nature. Strongly encouraged by the expanding colleges of education in the late 1960s, this form of environmental education prefers to deal with rural and historical environments and either ignores socio-political factors or treats them in a descriptive manner which emphasizes social consensus rather than conflict. Much use is made of such field study skills as village surveys and landscape drawing and while cognitive and aesthetic outcomes are stressed, there is a commonly held belief that environmental experience aids personal growth and moral development. Topic work creates school-community links and pupils may be encouraged to take part in such 'safe' action projects as litter collection or tree planting.

The widespread introduction of education *from* the environment into primary and middle schools was prompted by such texts as *Teaching Environmental Studies* (Lines and Bolwell, 1971), *Learning through the Environment* (Hopkins, 1968), and the *Approaches to Environmental Studies* series published by Blandford. It was given further credibility by the Schools Council's Environmental Studies 5–13 Project and the impact of this approach has been summarized by Selby.[6] While its influence in secondary schools has generally been confined to less able or reluctant pupils, many of the activities of the Art and the Built Environment Project are also in this tradition. This project does, however, represent an advance on earlier materials since it recognizes the complementary nature of education *from* and *for* the environment.

iii) Education for the environment is a combination of radical environmentalism and education which regards environmental well-being as its *goal*. The curriculum is designed to increase pupils' awareness of the moral and political decisions shaping their environment and to give them the knowledge, attitudes, and skills which will help them to form their own judgements and to participate in environmental politics. Such objectives are realized through issue-based projects in the immediate environment, which seek to cultivate awareness and understanding and culminate in some form of community action. The school is actively involved in the environmental issues facing the community, but the pupils' horizons are continually widened by examining comparable issues elsewhere in the world.

Major elements of education *for* the environment are present in only a minority of schools, but teachers wishing to explore its potential have a growing literature to guide them. The Town and Country Planning Association's education unit publishes the *Bulletin of Environmental Education (BEE)* which is a constant source of encouragement and radical ideas, and a special issue of *Undercurrents* on 'Children and the Environment' (No. 36, 1979) is a useful introduction to books and resources. *Education for Change* (Colin and Mog Ball, 1973) *Streetwork, the Exploding School* (Colin Ward and Tony Fyson, 1973), and *The Child in the City* (Colin Ward, 1979) are key texts for teachers wishing to rethink their approach, while relevant classroom material is to be found in *Utopia* (Colin Ward, 1974), *Planning your Environment* (Community Service Volunteers, 1976), *Caring for the Planet* (Robin Richardson, 1977), *People and Places* (Jay Farbstein and Min Kantrowitz, 1978), and *Up Your Street* (Youth Environmental Action, 1981). *Project Environment* (Schools Council/Longman, 1975), *Investigating Your Environment* (Biological

Sciences Curriculum Study/Addison Wesley, 1975), *Education for Neighbourhood Change* (Nottingham University, 1981), and *Art and the Built Environment* (Schools Council/Longman, 1982) are examples of curriculum projects which lead in radical directions. All these publications reflect a growing convergence of development, environmental, and community education as they attempt to counter the related symptoms of an unstable society.

It is highly unlikely that the environmental education found in any school or classroom will be a pure reflection of one of the three forms outlined above. Elements of all three will generally be found together and the curriculum will reflect the differing sources of ideas and materials on which teachers have drawn at different times. Many are often unaware of the social origins of the beliefs reflected in their chosen curriculum and even politically aware teachers will need to adapt their beliefs to the differing social systems and resources of their schools. All three forms of environmental education lead to claims that education promotes environmental quality, but only if there is adequate attention to education *for* the environment may such claims be thoroughly justified. Before examining how the geography teacher might attempt to implement this type of environmental education, we should consider the subject's recent record in this field.

Geography and environmental education

It is perhaps significant that the ecology movement and the new school geography emerged at almost the same time. The attractions of one diverted the attention of many geography teachers away from the other, and for the majority this meant that ideas and techniques relating to spatial analysis were given greater attention within the curriculum than those relating to ecology or environmental politics. As the 1970s progressed a more realistic balance between spatial and ecological analysis was achieved, but without a new attention to politics the dominant influence of these two forms of explanation was to strengthen the role of school geography as education *about* the environment. Some teachers did air utopian beliefs, especially when teaching about the developing world, but their messages about population explosions and resource crises simply reinforced the role of school geography as ideology. The lively debate about environmental ethics, education, and politics, which was so central to the mainstream of environmental education, engaged the attention of only a minority of geographical educators, and geography lessons in school were slow to incorporate the fundamental questioning of human-environment relations which was being encouraged elsewhere.

Environmental Geography (Keith Wheeler and Bryan Waites (eds.), 1976), was a significant attempt to revive neglected perspectives and some of its chapters deserved far more attention than they were given. Academic geographers were not so complacent as those in schools and their influence on the Schools Council 16–19 Geography Project now offers some hope that the debates within modern environmentalism will find their way into the classroom. It is hoped that this project's materials will strike a realistic balance between conventional and radical ideas.

The reader who wishes to glimpse something of the love-hate relationship between geography and environmental education in the 1970s should consult two Geographical Association reports.[7] Both outline the role of geography within environmental education, but while the earlier document bases the subject's claims on spatial analysis and key ideas, the more recent report adds ecological analysis, behavioural studies, decision-making, and aesthetics. It recommends the rational analysis of controversial issues in the classroom, but one senses that its proposals would rarely include the debate of utopian and radical alternatives to present realities, or lead to a fundamental questioning of the values on which our culture is based. This perception is reinforced by its unreserved plea that geography teachers co-operate with the environmental professions and so risk becoming party to the type of tokenism which currently pervades so much public participation in the planning field.

Not all geographers have been so cautious.[8] Shortle's early paper on environmental ethics and geographical education was a pioneering attempt to prompt a more relevant contribution and its message has gradually been explored in the literature. Some writers have fallen into the traps which utopian environmentalism offers, but there is now an emerging rationale whereby the geography curriculum may incorporate a fresh concern for environmental morality and politics.

Environmental ethics

A frequent claim made by environmentalists is that only ecology can provide the values and social ethics which will save us from impending disaster. Some conventionalists and most utopians argue that environmental imperatives should compel us to forget our current moral and political differences and allow the future to be shaped by ecological determinism. To this end, they have devised new codes of environmental ethics which emphasize respect for nature and natural principles and have suggested that these should be the basis of environmental education in schools. Such bold claims answer the professional needs of accommodators (Figure 14) and the psychological needs of utopians, but they are misguided and should be rejected.

A belief that 'nature knows best' reflects the philosophical error of regarding nature as an autonomous source of moral values and leads to codes of environmental ethics which conceal the political nature of environmental issues by claiming to represent the common interest. Their application would generally maintain or widen existing inequalities and it is prudent to regard most talk of environmental ethics as a conservative rather than radical response to environmental dilemmas.

If nature is not inherently 'good' or 'sacred', what foundations for environmental morality should we teach in schools? An answer is to be found in the realization that the environment frequently functions as an instrument of injustice and that our current exploitive attitudes towards nature seriously limit the options for other human beings, both living and yet to be born. By basing our appeals on justice and human rights rather than nature, we can begin to cultivate sound decision-making and behaviour on environmental issues. We will, however, remain open to charges of idealism unless we also recognize the material basis of human values and explore this in our lessons.

The geography curriculum should help pupils to understand the manner in which men and women make themselves and their environment in a two-way interaction with nature which is strongly conditioned by the kinds of lives they lead. Through case studies it should show that human labour may increase or decrease the carrying capacity and quality of the environment and that people's attitudes towards nature are shaped by prevailing forms of economic life with technology as a prime mediator. Appropriate attitudes of stewardship can only result from far-reaching changes in our material lives, for it is in these that social and human-environment relationships are founded. Appeals to justice and human rights remain idealistic unless we also seek to criticize the way in which we live.

Whilst socialist theory offers forms of economy and society which promise justice and environmental well-being for all, history shows us that in practice socialist planning does not end environmental abuse. The vast majority of capitalist and socialist governments currently maintain public support by fostering consumerism, a way of life which has inevitable consequences for the environment.[9] It is therefore no accident that soft technologists see the erosion of consumerism as a prerequisite to social and environmental reform.

Although everyone has a right to such basic needs as adequate housing, warmth, and healthy food, consumer societies are based on the manipulation of needs in order to sustain their economies and support for their rulers. Since possessions become the individual's major source of self-respect and the future is valued solely in terms of the hope it holds for fresh satisfactions, consumerism removes barriers to economic expansion and provides criteria whereby political policies may be judged. Sustained by powerful economic and political interests and entering almost every household via the television screen, consumer values are a root cause of ecological dangers and should be challenged. The geography teacher has frequent opportunities to do this.

Classroom implications

The majority of pupils we teach are continually making consumer decisions about such things as food, transport, clothing and entertainment. While these are often subconscious decisions, they frequently result in actions which sustain an economy based on environmental abuse. Junk food for tea maintains the conversion of Amazonia to beef ranches, is wasteful of packaging, and brings litter to the high street. A can of hair spray uses up precious metals and threatens the ozone layer. A short lift to school in the family car pollutes the air, congests the roads, and slows down the buses. Geography teachers have ready-made opportunities to examine the environmental impacts of such choices and help pupils to realize the wide-ranging costs which consumerism brings. A wide range of media may be used to evoke empathy towards those living in blighted environments, and the curriculum should also allow examination of communities which live in other ways and find greater fulfilment through more caring attitudes towards people and nature.

Relating curriculum content to pupils' personal lives and decisions in this way is a central aim of moral or values education. By encouraging values awareness, moral reasoning and development, empathy, and sound behaviour, values education can help pupils adopt a more critical yet constructive attitude to the world in which they live. It has been widely applied to environmental and social studies education in America and its techniques deserve wider use by geography teachers in Britain.[10] Not only can they make pupils more aware of the strong influence of consumerism on human lives and environments, but they can also prompt a search for viable alternatives which is likely to have major implications for schools as institutions.

The current power of consumerism is largely due to the dehumanizing work which most people are compelled to do. Consumer satisfactions are an appeasement for the lack of fulfilment which most work offers, yet are themselves inherently limited and temporary. If consumerism is to be undermined there must be radical changes in the nature of work to allow worker control, the end of alienated workplaces, and the emergence of alternative values. Jobs which require docility condition people for passive lives as consumers, whereas those which engage all workers in decision-making and offer human fulfilment allow the realization of ecologically sound futures. Radical environmentalists are just one group of activists working for such a transformation.

An analysis which links environmental well-being to the erosion of consumerism and the restoration of power to ordinary people requires us to acknowledge the present role of schooling in sustaining consumerism, docility, and powerlessness. If a curriculum which challenges conventional values is not simply to engender pessimism or suggest idealist solutions, teachers should not only help pupils to contemplate alternative forms of society and human-environment relations, but they should also ensure that pupils experience the rewards of self-determination in practice. In a pioneering book on environmental education, Mark Terry[11] suggested that schools should become model environments in which teachers and pupils live out their decisions and attempt to create a just and ecologically sound community. Energy and resources would be conserved, the school site would become a nature reserve or garden to enrich the pupils' lives, and community projects would gradually lead to change within the neighbourhood. His proposals have been implemented by a small number of radicals, but the majority of schools still condition pupils for passive roles in society and mirror the values of the world outside. If geography teachers are to challenge this correspondence between schooling and society in the interests of justice and the environment, they will need to give greater attention to values, school reform, and politics.

The opportunities for multinational companies selling junk foods, legislation against aerosol cans, the control of the private motorist in the local town, and the conversion of the school to a model environment are all dependent upon political decisions. Radical environmental education aims to give pupils the knowledge and ability to participate in politics and claim power with respect to the decisions which affect their own lives. Chapter 8 outlines a framework for political education in environmental decision-making and its adoption could bring a more critical and constructive approach to environmental issues in geography classrooms.

Future outlook

> 'But the fact remains that the kind of catastrophe forecast by the ecodoomsters in the sixties is more of a possibility now than it was then.'
> *Timothy O'Riordan*[12]

After a period of much curriculum development and growing interest amongst teachers, environmental education now claims less attention. Consultative documents urge greater support,[13] but political realities suggest that if further developments occur they will merely reinforce the present dominance of education *about* the environment. As environmental problems mount and the tensions between conventional and radical environmentalists grow, sensitive teachers and pupils will continue to seek alternative answers to mounting contradictions. With its critical approach to environmental ideologies and its attention to moral and political education, education *for* the environment can assist their search. Of the three forms of environmental education represented in schools, it is the only one which can facilitate a fundamental questioning of human values and political structures and so contribute to the transformation of society. Geographers who are prepared to use their classrooms as settings for such education will be making a valid contribution to environmental well-being and helping to avert the catastrophes to which O'Riordan refers. The environment is in a worse state than it was ten years ago and urgently requires our attention.

References

1 A. Gorz, *Ecology as Politics* (South End Press, 1980).
2 The discussion of environmental ideologies in this chapter draws upon:
   T. O'Riordan, 'Environmental ideologies', *Environment and Planning A*, 9 (1977).
   S. Cotgrove, 'Environmentalism and utopia', *The Sociological Review* (February 1976).
   F. Sandbach, *Environment, Ideology and Policy* (Blackwell, 1980).
3 T. O'Riordan, 'Environmental issues', *Progress in Human Geography*, 5, 3 (1981).
   Also see:
   T. O'Riordan, 'Environmentalism and education', *Journal of Geography in Higher Education*, 5, 1 (1981).
4 S. Sterling has compiled an annotated bibliography *Environmental Education in Theory and Practice* for the Council for Environmental

Education (University of Reading, London Road, Reading RG1 5AQ).

5   The origin of these labels is somewhat obscure, although the tensions between various interpretations of environmental education were clearly recognized by:
D. G. Watts, *Environmental Studies* (Routledge & Kegan Paul, 1969).
R. West, 'Environmental Education—some problems of definition and approach', *Bulletin of Environmental Education*, 46 (February 1975).
They have been discussed more recently by:
B. Goodey, 'The way in to environmental education', *Bulletin of Environmental Education*, 110 (June 1980).

6   C. Selby, 'Environmental studies in the middle years', *Trends in Education* (Winter 1977).

7   Geographical Association, *The Role of Geography in Environmental Education* (1974).
Environmental Education Working Group, 'Geography and environmental education: a discussion paper', *Teaching Geography* (July 1980).
A further perspective is provided by:
Scottish Association of Geography Teachers, *Geography and Environmental Education* (1977).

8   D. Shortle, 'Environmental ethics and geographical education', *Geography Teacher*, 11 (1971).
D. L. Smith, 'Values and the teaching of geography', *Geographical Education*, 3, 2 (1978)

9   My discussion of human needs and the replacement of consumerism owes much to:
A. L. Roberts, *The Self-managing Environment* (Allison & Busby, 1979).
K. Coates (ed.), *Socialism and the Environment* (Spokesman, 1972).

10 J. Huckle, 'Geography and values education', in R. Walford (ed.), *Signposts for Geography Teaching* (Longman, 1981).

11 M. Terry, *Teaching for Survival* (Ballantine, 1971)

12 T. O'Riordan, 'Environmental issues', *Progress in Human Geography*, 4, 3 (1980).

13 *Curriculum 11–16: Environmental Education*, HMI Consultative Document in Red Book Series (HMSO, 1979).
Environmental Education in Urban Areas, report by a working party of the Environmental Board of the Department of the Environment (HMSO, 1979).

Chapter 11

Urban studies

Chris Webb

It is strange just how vapid much educational discussion is in relation to the very dangerous globe that we inhabit. One has only to be outside mainstream curriculum debate for a very short time to marvel at the suspended theatre of a great deal of subject controversy. Schools often seem trapped in a moral aspic, most of the ingredients for which come from nineteenth-century cookbooks. The world's political and ecological systems are fracturing and yet no responsive urgency was reflected in the Great Debate, launched by the Ruskin College rhetoric of James Callaghan. Our cities are in a parlous state and a shrinking economy is transforming people's lives, yet Michael Rutter's[1] seminal research concentrates on the internal criteria of schooling. Racial conflict and the encroachment of the state on traditional civil liberties[2] are profound worries, and still the majority of schools persist in ordering their pupils in ways least designed to give them the experiences to grapple with these issues.

The problem that arises from this recognition has two implications. First, that any serious debate over the relationship between learning and the society within which it happens must develop new criteria for assessing and analysing this process. Without this it will remain a slightly incestuous, in-house dialogue which seems often both to echo and to amplify the social-control concerns of the early nineteenth century. Secondly, and this is the crux of the matter, a strategy of action for schools and education must be developed. At first sight this may appear either self-evident or even naive, but it is the area of 'doing' which has often been neglected by teachers and educationalists. Obviously the business of living in the world is a political thing and it is at this interface that words like 'democratic', 'just', or 'socialist' are shaped into a working reality. It is exactly here that most schooling has avoided contact and the school wall has been both a physical and metaphorical barrier. Schools are left as beached institutions, irrelevant to the issues that their pupils and their parents are submerged in. Bad housing, a deteriorating social fabric, unemployment, immobility, and a qualitatively poor environment are the lot of many people in our cities.

How does curriculum debate impinge on this or are the claims inherently fanciful and overblown? Is all the rhetoric concerning self-discovery and consciousness idealist in character, even when describing itself as concerned and socialist? It will only begin to avoid this charge when issues are both recognized and acted upon in the community of the school. This means a transformation in the historical posture of schools which often will be painful and political. It will mean opening up many new connections with the world in which both adult teachers and children live. It will mean extending pastoral concern into the state of housing, planning, employment, technology, and the rest. Equally, the curriculum itself, both in the narrow academic description and in its broadest operational sense, will extend into these areas of concern, collaboration, and conflict. This must be the context for debate about what and how to learn; otherwise the pervasive, institutional sterility of schooling will kill the initiative.

Notting Dale Urban Studies Centre

Environmental education has made many claims for itself, usually without addressing itself to any of the preceding arguments. It has become excessively dominated by architectural and planning idioms and, even worse, has begun to design an array of techniques intended to educate the perceptions. These often pre-empt any immediate reaction from people drawn from their own realities. The notion of urban studies centres has often been connected with the environmental lobby and, not surprisingly, those few which have been set up have tended to reflect the prevailing characteristics of schools in all but name. This has often meant publicizing a different subject focus as a potential agent of social change at the same time as holding onto notions of being a neutral venue. Effectively this both inflates and avoids the issues raised above so that the environmental education lobby often seems to be floating in a large, gas-filled balloon over the wasteland of our cities. The critical deficiency is in not having an educational critique. As Colin Ward[3] points out, 'there is an urban educational crisis because so many city children do not fit the style and method of the city's education system.' The converse being that the city itself (or the countryside) can be the learning medium through which one learns to use and, perhaps, control and change the environment. The problem is, can schools change?

At Notting Dale in west London we have been attempting to forge new connections and methods of work. This has been going on since 1974 and offers some experience to the arguments above. Our area was designated 'a plague spot' by Charles Dickens and the contemporary observer of high-rise follies, urban motorways, blight, and dumping would probably still agree with that description. But the juxtapositions are dramatic and one has to be purblind to avoid questions concerning allocation of space, wealth, opportunity, mobility, and ease. Most importantly one is looking at these issues with people who are both subjectively and objectively part of the landscape. This is surely the central characteristic of local studies which, in itself, challenges the orthodoxy of fact and the ways of arriving at knowledge. This has significant repercussions for teaching, learning, and evaluation. Even more significant are the demands it makes for action. How many years running does one catalogue and analyse the dearth of housing with groups of young people on the threshold of that market? Does one just record the structural and cyclical unemployment trends with young immigrants? Can the increasing dereliction of newly built housing estates merely be recorded as of visual interest or be understood as a public expenditure cut by young people who live there? All these examples, and many more, have their own imperative to expand understanding into action. If schools cared for their pupils in a serious and democratic way this could be a shared task. It will always be riddled with difficulty, local politics, and factions, but at least it would allow the school to be engaged with that world in which their pupils actually live.

For that to happen though, our experience suggests that the internal and external relationships with the community will have to be fundamentally different. It is also clear that any holistic notions of community are a romance and that the business of relating to the myriad factions, groups, and individuals of an area is a long and negotiated task. In fact this very simple idea of the time needed is often the death of school initiatives, given the weird, segmented, and frenetic routines so often created by timetable and habit.

The Notting Dale Centre has set up three main areas of work, all of which interrelate in quite fundamental ways. The whole notion is essentially eclectic, as that is how most intelligent adult beings are in the world. People rarely exist as geographers, flautists or whatever, but as conscious, expansive beings drawing on ranges of experience and information. This is not to deny particular subject-based contributions but to affirm the need for an integrated approach. Within such an approach the first and perhaps the most significant characteristic is that of being accessible, useful, and welcoming as a resource base. The second is that of being a diverse concentration of primary, urban materials for educational use, and the third is that of being an enabling agent, working with local groups on a range of issues. On the face of it a simple recipe, but the spectres of caretakers, insurance agents, timetablers, examiners, and other demands all militate against such simple provision within schools. Notting Dale, it is worth saying, is independent, which avoids some problems but raises a whole host of others. Not least among these is that the absence of traditional bogeymen (headmaster and local education authority) renders the normal apologia a trifle limp, but also lays bare the contradictions and failures more starkly.

London is a peculiarly intransigent place in terms of communications and, as a physical resource centre, Notting Dale has an important part to play in enabling people to communicate more effectively. Our local population is within four major bureaucracies consisting of two local boroughs, the Greater London Council, and, of course, the Government. All these have space, staff, some expertise, and time. It can take several years to get building maintenance done, let alone ascend the giddy heights of citizen participation. Within this, the business of giving people access to the machines and skills of communication becomes centrally important. Well over a hundred local groups use our offset-litho press, our photocopy machine, our graphic and typing skills. These groups range from tenants' groups, youth groups, action groups, through to local theatre companies, black organizations, church groups, and so on. How many schools will let adult strangers use their machines, their rooms, or skills? How many colleges would give a tenants' group a key to let themselves in to use the rooms for a meeting? E. P. Thompson in his essay 'The Segregation of Dissent' likened control of the media to 'mammoth turnpike trusts controlling the main arteries of communication'. Given this control, at a local level the resources of formal education could and should provide alternative means for people to engage political processes in both personal and organized ways.

These simple, enabling provisions can lead on to far more extensive, collaborative relationships with local people. Much of this takes time and is rarely as straightforward as those professional advocates of participation pretend, and certainly in our experience the formal and statutory attempts to involve people have either failed disastrously or whimpered away. This was often as much due to the simplistic and non-variable models presented by planners as to the differences in priorities and time-scales of the two sides. It was odd how close many of the statutory meetings were to bad, didactic teaching contexts, with information to be passed on rather than perceptions used and developed. But other relationships are possible and the implications of them formidable both for notions of local autonomy and for educational development. Two examples will suffice to illustrate this and in their various ways will underline the integral characteristic of local study and local involvement, and point out the implications for the redevelopment of part of the school curriculum and perhaps the whole of the ethos of schools.

The Edward Woods community project

Close to Notting Dale Centre is a dense, high-rise council estate known as the Edward Woods Estate. It was built on the edge of the M41 in the middle of the 1960s and is typical of the cliff-face follies of that era. It has an extraordinarily large proportion of old-age pensioners and single-parent families, which automatically renders most of the estate poor and immobile. The building technology is appalling, with a great deal of damp and the lifts of the 20-storey blocks constantly out of commission. This was home for a small group of fourteen-year-olds from a local school and, way back in 1975, they chose to focus on their estate as a local study. In many ways the archival and planning materials were more accessible than the population, and they spent some time putting together an account of the development of their home patch. They were astonished at the information they culled from the local census because they had no idea that the estate contained the bizarre population profile that it did. From this they decided to use video to portray the problems for old people on the estate and produced an extremely poig- nant tape of an old lady who lived on the eighteenth floor attempting to buy a bottle of milk. This was tantamount to cleaning out the Augean Stables, thanks to the hostility of so many architectural and technical features within those buildings.

The youngsters' initiative happened to coincide with a germinal tenants' association on the estate using Notting Dale to type out agendas and so on. The fact that this connection existed allowed their tape to be both seen and used by people at the Town Hall. From this very small beginning there grew up the Edward Woods community project, which embraced so many areas of debate within education, local politics, accountability, professional client relationships, participation and the rest, that in retrospect it is astonishing that it survived. It is worth emphasizing again that extensive and intensive involvement was the core of all this, very much at variance with the some-what ephemeral efflorescences of participation produced by the obligations raised under the Town and Country Planning Act (1972).

To attempt a narrative of the Edward Woods project would stretch this chapter into a whole book, so a brief description will suffice with the implications drawn out at some length. The work of school pupils on their home estate became a catalyst for movement within the tenants' association. In collaboration with Notting Dale it did a survey of the estate, published it as an attacking document, and held elections to form a committee to further the manifesto proposals. These three simple events took over a year and involved all kinds of people in new experiences and skills. In the next three years the elected group of mainly working-class mothers and staff at Notting Dale raised over £½ million, acquired land to build on, and started on a project to construct a multi-purpose hall to be built by unskilled, unem-ployed youngsters and to be managed by ourselves as both contractor and client. After many crises the hall was finished and is now at perhaps the most critical stage where new committees are being elected to develop its philos-ophy and practice.

Just before the building was finished a group of septuagenarians from the estate came on site and, looking right through the building that had been under construction in their midst for almost two years, they automatically assumed that the wooden site-hut was to be their new hall. This anecdote illustrates a very fundamental point concerning the pathetically low expecta-tions, both affective and cognitive, that almost all of us have with respect to controlling or shaping the environment.

The very real success of the building as a structure and a social opportunity can hide the many areas of difficulty and defeat. It is worth here positing some questions from this experience of self-build control and local autonomy. In terms of normal school relationships how does the business of pupils' work becoming part of political processes and evidence upset the status quo? Where does work for the community become involved in class or sectarian division and how do schools cope with that? Can schools as professional organizations cope with the democracy of collaboration and with knowledge as generated rather than given? How can professionals, be they architects, surveyors or engineers, communicate effectively with uneducated, lay groups? How far can rules of accountability be stretched or broken to allow real local control of financial resources? What is the balance, politically, between achieving ends more quickly with small groups and going through the convoluted processes of broad-based democracy and information channels? Could the project have worked at all without the consistent and persistent efforts of people at the Notting Dale Centre? If not, and it seems doubtful that it would have survived otherwise, what could be the implications for schools as partners in these and other kinds of ventures? How would they function with respect to other bureaucracies, not least their own employing bureaucracy?

These are just a few of the issues which might lurk behind a too facile usage of words like 'change', 'community', and 'participation'. They reflect a very local response to a local issue whereas the next example draws far more on macro-concerns and strategies for the future. But this kind of fluidity from the micro to the macro seems a characteristic of local study and its developments, which rescues it from the accusation of parochialism both in terms of knowledge and in terms of political action.

The technology centre

Unemployment is quite obviously going to become a larger problem, spawned by the supposed demands of efficiency and technology. This kind of industrial progress has been transformed into a universal principle which challenges the very heart of liberal notions regarding education. What exactly is a school or a subject meant to offer in an area of massive structural unemployment? What will be a positive reaction to the effects of the huge displacement of human labour through automation? Surely not that vision of a leisure society which appears to be the current palliative offering in this respect. A society busily recreating and educating itself seems a far cry from the workaday realities for most of our inner-city population. In Notting Dale, as in many parts of Britain and Europe, there is a population particularly vulnerable to recession, and figuring prominently within this are the young, both skilled and unskilled.

Obviously there is an immediate sense of tragedy in the bleakness of opportunity for the young and on one level a massive effort must be made politically and economically to ensure that reasonable work is available. But more importantly, a new vision of production and control is needed, embedded in different notions of organization and value. At Notting Dale we have set up in the last year a technology centre which is attempting to become a model for a more human-centred and socially responsible organization of technology and production. It has three basic areas, two of which are already functioning and one which is being developed now. First, it is a training centre for young, unemployed people who want to learn about computers, microprocessors, and electronics. There are no entry requirements and the educational philosophy is the simple one of learning by doing. Personal projects and self-direction characterize the learning process and reflect the social ambience of the place. The very business of attempting this with the 'failures' of the schooling system has laid bare the inadequacies of current developments within computer and electronics education which will have to be remedied internally by the creation of new materials and techniques. The immediate reason for this part of the technology centre is to attempt to meet the aspirations of the young unemployed and to make them both skilful in and aware of the new technologies. In many ways this can be seen as a Faustian pact and this is why the centre has other developmental aims, focused on the intermediate future.

To further these ideas a microprocessor development and research unit has been set up. This has pressed on with advances in microprocessor education, prototype development, and problem solving. It faces two ways in these respects. For the training centre it provides solutions, programmes, and real manufacturing contexts for the young people by concentrating on areas of need rather than just those things which are profitable. There are obviously many such markets of need and we have concentrated on one. The problems of disabled people can sometimes be met by sensitively constructed machinery; microprocessors, being programmable and miniature, are an extremely useful addition here. But to be useful to disabled people the young trainees will have to spend time with them, as well as problem solving and constructing devices. The effect of this is a net increase in labour requirement using the new technologies for socially useful ends, often on just a break-even basis financially.

The other face of the research unit is its attempt to float small businesses out of these experiences so that a network of employment is developed on a locally controlled level. Some parts can be profitable and others subsidized by that profit, so that the expensive needs of labour-intensive problems can be met. This seems to us to provide a coherent model for the relationship between learning, work, and the real needs of the society within which it is all based. It also attempts to demystify the whole 'blackbox' characteristic of science and technology by making it physically accessible and socially reponsible.

Such things may seem a far cry from urban environmental education, but they are not if you address yourself to the substantive issues that such work will uncover. The above example has grown out of a local analysis linked to a broader-based perspective. In concrete terms it exists within a huge network of relationships ranging through central and local government, universities and polytechnics, trade unions, industry, trusts, a variety of national organizations, and a whole crowd of sympathetic teachers, scientists and individuals. Such a reformed concept of education will challenge the typical isolation of schools on all kinds of financial, legal, and historical levels. But think what internal implications for school and subject organization there could be through such a development. The whole range of science, design, and technology would have a part to play, as would the geographers, sociologists, and economists. The school curriculum as an ongoing activity could be purposefully exploded into a local venture. Within this, both adults and youth could learn, produce, and collaborate. The real, socially constructed relationship between theory and practice could satisfy many different aspects of the educational model, ranging from the purely academic to vocational utility. But any such sharing of resources will threaten much of the pseudo-professional characteristic of teaching. For survival, if not for ideals, this threat will have to be faced, and subject arguments at least conducted within the parameters outlined.

Issues and action

Obviously for many within education the two cases described above are in unfamiliar territory. In this last section the work of Notting Dale Urban Studies Centre will be discussed within the more familiar range of urban and environmental work. As a centre it hosts both formally and informally a whole range of educational users, ranging across age and ability groups from primary to post-graduate and adult education and across subject boundaries as diverse as English, drama, sociology, history, geography, science, art, architecture, planning, and landscape design. Interestingly enough we offer much the same kind of educational possibilities to all these different groups. These break down into provision of physical resources and space, access to primary materials and the local environment and, finally, a working ethos within our social organization.

It is an issue-based and action-oriented perspective that we adopt and one which is best defined as a form of political education which draws upon a host of methods and subjects for its intelligence. The concomitant of this is that we have to be richly equipped and resourced so that investigative and generative work can be conducted. In this respect the centre has a very wide range of archival material concerning our part of west London. Maps, photographs, slides, historical documentation, oral histories, planning and architectural material, local government minutes, official documentation, and case studies constitute the bulk of this.

Basically we are concerned to enable people to penetrate, understand, and perhaps act upon their environment both locally and globally. Such inflated designs often preface curriculum description and our experience is, increasingly, that the way in which this learning is done is just as important, if not more so, than the actual issues, facts, and accounts that are approached and generated. This relates to our experience of working within the locality; if the possibilities of participation and collaboration are to be realized, then the learning process must, in its own right, contain those same experiences of autonomy, collaboration, and self-generation. What can such words mean for children and adults?

Autonomy can be the experience for a group of fourth-year school students of both choosing and managing their own research aims and methods. It can be the business of learning how to process film, use a duplicator, or develop other such skills in a way that makes a person independent. Or, more radically, it can be the experience of young people working with adults on issues within their own locality and perceptions. In this case the notion that their everyday knowledge is important and relevant is liberating in contradistinction to the heavy structures which schools and examinations present as received wisdom. In the same way the experience of working collaboratively can be an unusual and fruitful experience for those raised within the individualistic tenor of examinable knowledge.[4] This can be reflected by a group of in-service teachers researching and producing oral histories of their borough and in the process picking up a range of skills. It is strange how often adults within education are diffident and nervous of other fields of knowledge, almost as if the subject demarcations produced no-go areas. As for a word like 'generative', this begins to describe the process whereby a group of ten-year olds can make visible, by their investigations, accounts of their local estate and the views of its pensioner population. This is knowledge in the making and although partial it can command a position in the market-place of explanations. In this sense environmental education can be fundamentally democratic and any child brings a lifetime of experience to bear in a way that more formal subjects often preclude. The challenge lies in the inbuilt difficulty of much relevant resource material. How can young and old alike have both physical access to and understanding of accounts that are often purposefully opaque or reflect the linguistic camouflage of different professional groups? The 'soft city'[5] of perceptions and dreams is available, but the 'hard city' has high walls and impressive defensive strategies.

To attempt to breach these fortifications, urban and environmental education should be:

i) exploratory and action-based, using the environment, particularly of the city, as a resource;

ii) eclectic in its approach, employing all that is best in a range of subject perspectives and methods;

iii) critical in its attempts to relate the different perspectives (stucco may be decorative but why ten door-bells up the side of the door?);

iv) democratic in its fundamental reliance on the working perceptions of people as its base;

v) political in its concern to understand why things are as they are—cities, particularly, reflect distribution of all things, be they space, health, housing, jobs, or wealth;

vi) actively futuristic, for if the above characteristics do not produce some kind of reaction, environmental education will have dug its own grave.

This may well sound unduly dramatic, but the world we live in is bleak in prospect and, if urban studies cuts itself off from its own root causes, it will render itself both impotent and unimportant.

If educationalists are to make claims for a particular subject as an agent of social and moral change, then they must beware of hyperbole and self-delusion. Only by extending their arguments into a more comprehensive critique of society, schooling and, in particular, their own institutions, will they be able to develop a view of the problems that face them. Moral exhortations for a better and more just world will not help if the organizational inertia of school and classroom resists the pressures from outside. The world is in a state of crisis and it is time that educational arguments faced that fact, rather than looking backwards to the Never-Never Land of 'lost standards' or forwards to the New Renaissance. It really is time to grow up—we have many shoulders to stand on.

References

1 M. Rutter *et al.*, *Five Thousand Hours* (Open Books, 1979).
2 E. P. Thompson, 'The state of the nation', in *Writings by Candlelight* (Merlin, 1980).
   S. Hall, *Drifting into a Law and Order Society* (The Cobden Trust, 1979).
3 C. Ward, *The Child in the City* (Architectural Press, 1977).
4 M. F. D. Young, *Knowledge and Control* (Collier Macmillan, 1971).
5 J. Raban, *Soft City* (Fontana, 1974).

Section C **Prospect**

'But the question "Why am I a teacher, anyway?" also produces
answers that are encouraging: for example, that one can participate
in the making of intelligence and, thereby, in the development of a
decent society. As soon as a teacher recognizes that this is, in fact, the
reason he became a teacher, then the subversion of our educational
system strikes him as a necessity.'
Neil Postman and Charles Weingartner, 1971

'. . . one of the key aims of education for justice must be to
encourage the development of critical consciousness, so that people
emerge from their silence, find their voice, and become fully
conscious subjects, capable of trying to change the conditions in
which they live.'
Brian Wren, 1977

'If, then, schools are to be used in the context of political struggle, an
explicit link has to be made between education and the future—the
content of education has to be given socialist (and not just capitalist)
relevance. . . . It is necessary to make education relevant in a new
way and for an alternative future.'
Simon Frith and Paul Corrigan, 1977

'There are a number of positions on the curriculum. The
back-to-basics, needs-of-industry lobby and the education-
for-leisure people have a lot in common. Both narrow the
curriculum, favour the status quo and downgrade social understanding and criticism. Paradoxically, the actual developments
taking place in schools are *widening* the curriculum: equal
opportunity for boys and girls, multicultural education, world
development education, media studies, etc. All these curriculum
changes provide opportunities for radical teachers to use them to
advantage.'
Editorial in *Teaching London Kids*, No. 16

Chapter 12

Daring to be a teacher

Robin Richardson

'Forgive me', he wrote. 'On two counts. One, that I have replied so late to your invitation to the weekend meeting at Birmingham on "The School in a World of Change". That you can put down to bad manners. Two, that I'm going to decline your kind invite. That you can put down to disillusionment.'

Brian, who wrote this letter, is a teacher of geography and social studies. The conference to which he had been invited, and to which he had decided not to come, was to do with the relationship between education and social change, with particular regard to questions of social justice and injustice in the wider world and to the role of the individual classroom teacher in teaching about such questions. Brian's letter continued: 'I agree with the whole ethos of the meeting at Birmingham and I'm sure it's just the pick-me-up I need. But at the moment I'm afraid I could not bear to hear new ideas of any import—the net result at the moment would be a feeling of guilt, incompetence, and relative deprivation. It's a long story, but I feel frustrated in the job and the only way I feel I'm going is backwards. . . . The doldrums! Feet in molasses! But please don't see this in any other way than a passing gloom. It's just a question of trying to work out what I've got to do—gird the old loins and not take on anything at the moment that comes under the category of effort. I'm sorry. Brian.'

No doubt many readers of this book can readily sympathize. They know at first hand, and day by dreary day, the hassles, tensions, and disappointments of classroom teaching: the sense of seldom finishing anything satisfactorily; the need to co-operate with, or at least to work alongside, colleagues with whom one has little or no ideology in common; the assault on one's personal maturity which is mounted hour by hour by large classes of adolescents; the pressure to be tidy, to take things easy, to narrow and blur one's gaze, to assent uncomplaining to the conventional wisdom that the best is the enemy of the good; the urge not to rock the boat, not to ask awkward questions, not to risk pain or damage, or sniping or ridicule; the absence of time and space for reflection, deliberation, weighing pros and cons, sorting out one's experience; the dull knowledge that a certain minimal efficiency—making and setting work, communicating with colleagues and parents, seeing to trivial problems—is a duty, not a virtue. 'A man digging knee-deep in a muddy ditch', it was once suggested, with banks so high as to shut out the landscape, in a hot sun, and with a permanent swarm of flies and gnats round his head, is no unfair description of the life of many a deserving teacher.'[1] Yes.

However, we do also have other feelings and experiences. It is reasonable, if we wish to be supportive of Brian and to help ourselves when we share the mood in which he wrote that letter, to ask about these other feelings and experiences, and to sort them out. Can we draw up a list, however rough and ready, of what Brian needs: as an individual teacher, as an individual person? Such a list would be useful as we plan, or at least wonder about, our reactions and responses to this book. What do we propose to look for in our further reading, for example, and in the in-service courses and workshops which we shall be attending or arranging, and in the conversations and discussions which we shall be having with colleagues and friends? What, in the light and context of this book, do we hope to pick up and develop from our daily experience in the weeks, months, years, ahead?

The list to be outlined in this chapter has four main items: techniques of teaching; skills of teaching; certain values and attitudes; political skills. The chapter is also concerned, of course, with theoretical understanding. But this latter concern is mainly implicit. Most of the other chapters are to do with the theoretical understanding which Brian and other teachers need: it is more important here to focus on the skills and values with which understanding has to be accompanied if it is to be effective. Understanding does, however, feature in Figure 16, which is a graphic summary of the chapter as a whole.

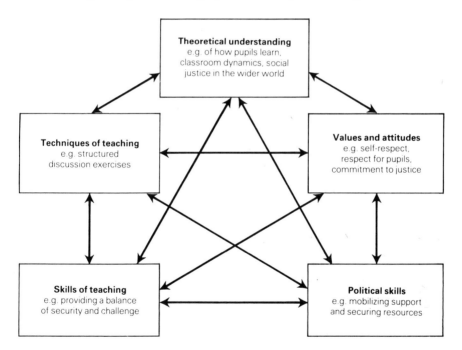

Fig. 16 A visual summary of Chapter 12. The arrows emphasize that each element in the model influences, and is influenced by, each of the others. The two-way relationships between techniques and skills of teaching, and between skills and values, are particularly discussed in the chapter.

Techniques of teaching

With regard to the first item, the point is simple and obvious, yet difficult to overemphasize. As a teacher you need to possess a wide repertoire of techniques. You need to be able, without expending a great deal of emotional energy, and without having to concentrate very hard, to get your pupils to sit up and take an interest—introspectively in themselves, mutually in each other, and objectively in social justice itself. The techniques you need have little or nothing to do with are 'bwops' (blackboards, worksheets, and overhead projectors) or the kind of teacher talk (telling, lecturing, instructing, ordering, correcting, criticizing) with which bwops are typically accompanied. Rather, the necessary techniques are to do with pupil talk: ways and means of ensuring that pupils learn through constructive talk with each other. The alternative to bwops and teacher talk is not mere desultory chat by the pupils, it is not merely the swapping of anecdotes and of uninformed and unexamined opinions. This point has been made well at the level of abstract theory by, for example, the Bullock Report: 'In order to accept what is offered when we are told something, we have to have somewhere to put it; and having somewhere to put it means that the framework of past knowledge and experience into which it must fit is adequate as a means of interpreting and apprehending it . . . The development of this individual context for a new piece of information, the forging of links that give it meaning, is a task that we customarily tackle by talking to other people . . . Important among the teacher's purposes should be the intention to increase the complexity of the children's thinking, so that they do not rest on the mere expression of opinion but use language in an exploratory way . . . The teacher must devise situations in which the pupil . . . becomes positively aware of the need for a complicated utterance, and is impelled to make it.[2]

The abstract theory of the Bullock Report has to be reflected and embodied in, amongst other things, practical techniques. To put it simply, the teacher needs a repertoire of structured discussion exercises for small groups. The repertoire can be extended and enriched partly by consulting handbooks, for example those which are mentioned in the notes at the end of this chapter;[3] more importantly, of course, it is a matter of actually experiencing such exercises as a participant, for example at in-service courses and workshops, not just of reading about them; most importantly of all, the repertoire is developed through practical trial and error in one's own classroom, and through careful reflection on what goes well and what badly. Here is a brief checklist which can be used at in-service courses and workshops, and in personal deliberations, to identify some of the main points to look for when selecting and designing discussion exercises:

i) *Things to handle*. Arrange for pupils to work with things which are tangible—objects, pictures, slips of paper, which they can handle.

ii) *Precise task*. Give precise, unambiguous instructions about the actual outcome you want. For example: 'Here are pictures of six different people. Choose the two people you would most like to meet. For each of them, write down two questions you would most like to put to them.'

iii) *Co-operation*. Give tasks which require pupils to listen to each other and to help each other, and which cannot be achieved unless everyone plays an active part. For example, use jigsaw exercises: a piece of written or visual material is cut up and has to be reassembled, but no pupil can see anyone else's fragment(s) during the preliminary description and discussion.

iv) *Small groups*. The smaller the group, the more secure pupils feel—they are less anxious about looking or feeling ridiculous, or making a mistake. Also, of course, the smaller the group the more everyone can talk. Often arrange for pupils to work in twos or threes. The maximum for most group work is six.

v) *Controversy*. Choose subjects on which pupils are likely to have conflicting opinions. Or build controversy into a discussion by requiring pupils to play simple roles.

vi) *Non-verbal material*. Use material which communicates ideas symbolically and non-verbally as well as by words—photographs, cartoons, posters, diagrams, charts. Let the pupils express themselves in these ways too.

vii) *Comparing, contrasting, selecting, justifying*. Provide a collection of items (pictures, quotations, newscuttings, actual objects) to be compared and contrasted with each other. Ask the pupils to arrange them or select from them, and justify their arrangement or selection.

viii) *Activity followed by reflection*. Give the pupils an activity to perform, or let them watch an activity—for example, a non-verbal game or exercise. Then have discussion and clarification of what happened, and of how they felt, and of what can be learnt.

ix) *Not too easy, not too hard*. Definitely reckon to stretch the pupils with the discussion tasks you set. But don't depress them or annoy them by providing tasks which are too difficult. When you fail, as you sometimes will, to get the balance right, let pupils discuss how they feel.

Skills of teaching

The second item which teachers need is skills of teaching, as distinct from techniques. It was risky and provocative to start the list here with reference to techniques, as if they are more important than the teacher's knowledge of why and how to use them, and of his/her purposes and attitudes. But equally it would have been misleading, if less unconventional, to start the list with an emphasis on skills and intuition. For there is a dialectical relationship between techniques on the one hand and skills on the other. Neither always precedes the other: skills generate and inform techniques, but techniques also develop skills. This point is recalled by the two-way arrows in Figure 16. But what, in the present context, is the distinction which is being proposed?

Techniques can be picked up from reading a handbook or from attending an in-service workshop, but skills come only from experience, and from reflection on experience. They can be described in words, but cannot be communicated through words alone. In the same way that you cannot become an expert doctor or art dealer simply by reading textbooks, so also you cannot become a more skilled teacher simply by reading or hearing this:

'I listen as carefully, accurately, and sensitively as I am able to each individual who expresses himself. Whether the utterance is superficial or significant, I listen. To me the individual who speaks is worthwhile, worth understanding . . . I wish very much to make the climate psychologically safe for the individual. I want him to feel from the first that if he risks saying something highly personal, or absurd, or hostile, or cynical, there will be at least one person in the circle who respects him enough to hear him clearly and listen to that statement as an authentic expression of himself . . . I am well aware that one cannot make the experience safe from the pain of new insight or growth, or the pain of honest feedback from others. However, I would like the individual to feel that whatever happens to him or within him I will be psychologically very much with him in moments of pain or joy, or the combination of the two which is such a frequent mark of growth . . . I trust the feelings, words, impulses, fantasies, that emerge in me. In this way I am using more than my conscious self, drawing on some of the capacities of my whole organism . . . A colleague has told me that I "peel my own onion", that is, express continuously deeper layers of feeling as I become aware of them in a group. I can only hope that this is true.'[4]

We are a long way, when reading such words, from mere tricks and gimmicks, from mere techniques. Nevertheless, such skills are developed over the years from experience, not from reading or listening, and such experience has to be, amongst other things, of using techniques. To repeat: techniques and skills are complementary. It will be important here in due course to consider in some detail how teachers can be helped to develop such skills.

Values and attitudes

But first it is relevant to turn to the third item in our list, which is to do with values and attitudes. For whatever assistance can and should be given to teachers to help them develop skills must also aim to develop values and attitudes as well. The quotation above, certainly, shows that teaching skills are closely allied not only to theoretical understanding of individual and group psychology but also to attitudes towards the pupils and towards oneself. For example, there is the educator's respect for the learners; his concern for them and his desire to empathize with them; his trust in his own feelings; his high self-esteem, yet also his docile curiosity, his openness to hear new ideas and viewpoints, his preparedness to take risks. Some of these values and attitudes are reflected also in the following passage, which is from an analysis of radicalism both as a personal lifestyle and as a political ideology. The stance which is described here is one with which the radical teacher goes often into the classroom, and into conversations and discussions in the staffroom. Also, it is a stance which he or she hopes and intends to see develop in pupils:

'Suppose that I am trying to convey to a friend the value I see in a new social policy. In order to comprehend how it is impinging upon his needs and interests I must temporarily suspend the structure of meanings that it has for me and imagine myself in his place. I must do this in spite of the frightening consequences for myself. The risk I undertake is permitting my structure to crumble, with the knowledge that a new element supplied by him may prevent the logical restructuring of my beloved ideas. I risk being ridiculed by him at a moment when my competence is not firmly in my grasp. By investing my undefended worth I am risking the verdict that I am worthless. I tell him something which shows that I value his judgement but leave him free to disconfirm and devalue my judgement and so alter the definition of our relationship. I do this because I am seeking confirmation from him and the expansion of my ideas—yet I cannot gain these without temporarily "surrendering" and risking permanent loss.'[5]

The same author cites not only self-criticism and respect for opponents as defining characteristics of the true radical but also the following, amongst others: 'he can stare into the face of injustice and absurdity without yielding in determination to balance and make it just, . . . he fashions periodically new and daring facets to his identity, which he examines and understands, . . . he forever seeks fresh and greater competence for himself, . . . he invests and commits himself to others authentically and intensely;' and, most importantly of all, 'he bridges the great distances to the deviant, the despised, the minority groups, and the "enemies" of his country, to make contact, to bring compassion, and discover novel life.'[6]

The key questions are how can teachers be inspired and supported to adopt a radical style of living and working along such lines, and how can they be helped to develop skills in the classroom so that their pupils are likely to adopt in due course a similar style themselves. One answer is through in-service workshops and courses of a certain kind—of the kind evoked by the quotations which follow. They are from comments by teachers about a conference which they had attended on multi-ethnic education.[7]

'Something basic has happened to me, I think! Will it be sustained? I am going to make a promise to myself to cut down on talking and increase my listening—that could be very significant.'

'The key to it all was the way of working. No lectures, no experts. All course members were free to show initiative and responsibility. Result: energy flowed, insights came, understanding developed, friendships were made.'

'The big question for me . . . will be where do we go from here and how? I'd like to think that the powers that be (that weren't here and won't know how good and unique it was) would be putting their heads together to see how the local authority could support and promote this tender but powerful initiative from the teachers whose lives they are appointed to nurture. I only hope they won't be worried by any possible political implications (big and little p, educational and social). I'm sceptical that this weekend will lead to much. But it did feel like the road to Damascus. So who knows?'

The occasion was built around structured discussion exercises: not around lectures, and not around the desultory conversations which are all too often at in-service courses and conferences misnamed as 'discussion', with immense and untold damage in due course to children and young people as the ripples move onwards into classrooms. At the very least, the teachers at this conference are likely to have picked up some useful techniques. Their comments, however, suggest that they may have learnt more than mere techniques. It will be useful and relevant to try to identify here in closer detail how the use of structured discussion exercises at an in-service course can help teachers develop skills as well as techniques, and new or modified values and attitudes.

The first aspect of structured discussion exercises, as distinct from lectures and from aimless, point-scoring conversations, is that they give participants a sense of their own value. Participants feel that they are perceived as resources from whom others may learn, and that their previous knowledge and experience is valid and relevant. They are perceived and respected as centres of consciousness—subjects who can say 'I', with wishes, intentions, hopes, ideals: not objects to be manipulated, not empty vessels to be given inputs (this common term betrays a terrible poverty of understanding and respect on the part of so many conference organizers), not merely an audience to be impressed or instructed or entertained. They feel that they are perceived and valued by the conference organizers and other participants not primarily as teachers who happen to be human beings, but as creative, responsible, self-directing, self-managing human beings who choose to be teachers. This perception corresponds to their own deepest self-perception, and they feel secure and invigorated.[8] The stage is set for learning by this climate of trust and security. There is a moral culture of reasonableness, orderliness, truthfulness, freedom, and respect for persons.[9]

Or rather, there are the outward and visible signs of such a moral culture. The inner reality is not necessarily present, there are not necessarily objective grounds for participants to feel that they are perceived and valued as centres of consciousness and relevant experience. It *could* all be a trick or a sham. The point to emphasize is that the rules of a structured discussion exercise (as also incidentally, the rules of procedure in political assemblies, committees and parliaments) have the same relationship to moral culture as do good manners and common courtesies to morality in interpersonal relationships. The outward form is both a symbol and an inspiration, both a sign and a signpost: it points to inner, invisible, moral feelings which both may be and should be present. Techniques, to recall and repeat, can generate and strengthen skills. Similarly the rules of a little playful discussion exercise can inspire and reinforce qualities of orderliness, truthfulness, equality, respect for persons, and so on. It is important to recall this basic dialectic between outward appearance and inner reality, form and content, rule and morality, in the following discussion of a number of further points about structured discussion exercises.

Discussion exercises not only prepare the way for learning by providing participants with a sense of security and respect from others. They also require participants actually to practise certain skills and to adopt certain attitudes. In other words they teach through activity—rather as someone might be taught through activity, as distinct from being instructed in words alone, to keep his balance on a bicycle. They practise the skill of listening, for example—paying close attention to what a handful of other people say, not interrupting, not pigeon-holing, not dismissing prematurely, not scoring points. They practise also other skills of small group discussion: clarifying, summarizing, supporting, seeking new information and viewpoints. Further they adopt certain attitudes—they see the other participants as centres of consciousness, subjects who say 'I', persons to be respected—and they have greater trust in their own feelings.

Feeling secure because they are themselves attended to and valued, yet also stimulated and challenged because they attend to and value others, the participants in a workshop built around discussion exercises unfreeze their minds: they consider new or more complex explanations of themselves and of their world, and they admit (inwardly or, more effectively, in speech) to tensions and inconsistencies in their own thinking and feeling. This unfreezing involves redrawing the boundary between the two main elements, personal freedom and outward constraint, in that old prayer: 'Grant me the courage to change what I can change; serenity to accept what I cannot; and wisdom to know the difference.' Unfreezing of the mind is the beginning and the underpinning of this wisdom. Over and over again, in the kind of in-service occasion being evoked and outlined here, teachers discover that in certain respects they are freer than they thought they were. For example, they find that they can empathize with the youthfulness of their pupils, and can be more tolerant and more patient with them, as a result of acknowledging cheerfully that there are still immaturities and muddles within themselves. By owning some of their own inadequacies, as distinct from denying them and projecting them onto their pupils, they find that they are freer in their classrooms to give freedom. 'Something basic has happened to me,' said one of the teachers quoted earlier, 'I am going to make a promise to myself to cut down on talking and increase my listening.'

Teachers can also be heartened at this kind of workshop to realize that there are certain outward constraints about which, at least in the short term, they can do nothing. Therefore they no longer blame themselves for things which are actually not their fault, but in the nature of the overall educational and political system. Brian, quoted at the start of this chapter, expected that the conference to which he had been invited would give him feelings of guilt, incompetence, and relative deprivation. So it might have done, that is precisely the effect of too many in-service courses and conferences, even though few teachers register their disapproval and rejection as firmly as Brian. But in-service courses are not inherently demoralizing. Brian might have found that he is far more skilled, and far more free to exercise his skills and to promote analogous skills in his pupils, than he imagined.

Political skills

The moral culture which is symbolized and in part built by structured discussion exercises can, and ought to, be present in both in-service courses and school classrooms. That is the fundamental point which is being re-hearsed and illustrated in this chapter. In so far as it is indeed present in both those places, then geography teachers like Brian will feel less often discouraged and demoralized, and will be more likely to act on the ideas and proposals about geography teaching outlined elsewhere in this book. However, the same moral culture needs also to be present in other places: in the geography or humanities department as a whole, and in the school as a whole; and in relationships between a school and the parents of its pupils, and between a school and the local community more generally. In order to sustain the moral culture in these other places teachers need political skills. These include the capacity to identify other people's material and psychological interests, in particular their concerns about status, power, territory, and money; the capacity therefore to mobilize support for one's own proposals and practices, using different arguments and slants as appropriate; and equally the capacity to anticipate opposition from a variety of quarters, and to dispel it, divert it, or disarm it; the capacity in consequence to secure scarce resources—funds, equipment, time, space and territory, status—to protect and promote what one wishes to do. Such political skills are merely machiavellian and manipulative if they are unaccompanied by genuine respect for the other people with whom one is working. But there is no reason in principle why they should not be so accompanied. In any case respect for others is often a fragile or even futile value if it is not in its turn accompanied by political skills.

Acknowledging oneself as a teacher

To summarize and conclude. A teacher of geography who reads and sympathizes with the other chapters in this book, and who wishes and intends to act on them, or to continue acting on them, is likely to be able to say some or all of the following: 'I am a teacher more than a geographer, and a person more than a teacher. I seek to widen the repertoire of techniques I use in the classroom to enable my pupils to grow as persons, talking thoughtfully and respectfully to each other, for I look to their growing commitment to social justice. I hope to extend not only my techniques of teaching but also my skills, so that there is an optimum balance in my classroom of security and challenge. I aspire to deepen my tolerance and my commitment to justice, both in my immediate situation and in the wider world. I seek opportunities for such learning, and moral support, at in-service courses of various kinds. I reckon to improve my political skills, particularly within and around the school where I teach. I recognize that Brian, quoted at the start of this chapter, speaks for me in some of my moods; but I have other moods also. In these I am a self-managing human being who dares—yes, who dares—to be a teacher.'

Something like that. At the least in a quiet murmur or whisper. Better still, out loud.

References

1 Edward Thring, the nineteenth-century headmaster, quoted in W. A. Reid, *Thinking about the Curriculum* (Routledge & Kegan Paul, 1978), p. 15.
2 *A Language for Life* (HMSO, 1975), paragraphs 4.9 and 10.11.
3 In the United States a seminal handbook of the 1970s was:
S. Simon, K. Howe, H. Kirschenbaum, *Values Clarification—a Handbook of Practical Strategies for Teachers and Students* (Hart Publishing Co., 1972). Most of its exercises can be adapted to the subject-matter of geography. More immediately relevant for geography are the two handbooks compiled by the World Studies Project: *Learning for Change in World Society: Reflections, Activities, Resources* (1976) and *Debate and Decision: Schools in a World of Change* (1979). Also the various games and exercises published by Oxfam and Community Service Volunteers.
There are many excellent practical ideas, adaptable for almost any school subject, in various handbooks concerned with language development and English as a foreign or second language; one of the best is:
D. Byrne and S. Rixon, *Communication Games* (NFER Publishing Co., 1979). There are in addition some simple but useful ideas, with transcripts of pupils using them, in:
D. Barnes and F. Todd, *Communication and Learning in Small Groups* (Routledge & Kegan Paul, 1977).
4 Quotations from the chapter entitled 'Can I be a facilitative person in a group?' in C. Rogers, *Encounter Groups* (Allen Lane, 1971).
5 C. Hampden-Turner, *Radical Man* (Duckworth, 1971), p. 48.
6 Ibid, p. 60.
7 The conference was organized by Lewisham Teacher's Centre in 1980, and was based on exercises published in *Debate and Decision: Schools in a World of Change* (World Studies Project, 1979).
8 For a comprehensive technical discussion of changes in self-concepts, roles, behaviour, values, attitudes, see:
R. Ziller, 'A helical theory of personal change', in R. Harré (ed.), *Personality* (Blackwell, 1976).
9 The terminology here is taken from a very interesting and useful philosophical analysis of group discussion as a way of teaching:
D. Bridges, *Education, Democracy and Discussion* (NFER Publishing Co., 1979), pp. 20–6.

Chapter 13

The geography curriculum in the 1980s

Michael Storm

How much geography will be taught in the 1980s? What kind of geography will it be? Who will teach it, and to whom? The only thing one can confidently assert is that the answers to these questions will not, on the whole, be provided by school geography teachers.

Any attempt to chart likely developments within the next ten years must necessarily start with a few reminders of the external constraints affecting the school curriculum as a whole, and geography's position within the curriculum. A review of constraints must start with the transformed demographic context of secondary and higher education. In 1977 there were 3.7 million pupils in compulsory secondary education in England and Wales; by 1991 there may be as few as 2.5 million. This basic trend, reinforced by the non-materialization of the surge in staying-on predicted in the early 1970s, may well produce an absolute decline in numbers in sixth forms, further and higher education by the end of the 1980s. The geography of falling rolls is currently being investigated by an eminent geographer/administrator Dr Eric Briault,[1] whose findings remind us that population dynamics and age structures vary dramatically, producing rising school populations in some localities. Nevertheless, it is useful to consider school geography in the 1980s against this background of falling rolls, since an exclusive preoccupation with paradigms and ideologies within the subject sometimes calls to mind Schumacher's classic metaphor about the careful arranging of deckchairs on the deck of the Titanic.

Curriculum rationalization

Thus, logistical imperatives are requiring schools to re-examine the range of subject choice offered in years four and five of the secondary course. An HMI survey[2] identified no less than sixty subjects on offer, with a typical options list of nineteen to twenty-four. The evident move towards a more substantial compulsory core (averaging 47 per cent of total provision, according to the HMI survey, but varying from 23 per cent to 93 per cent of pupil time in schools at either end of the range) owes little to philosophical or political debate but rather represents a recognition of resource constraints. If more upper school curriculum content is to be incorporated in a compulsory core, there is a powerful case for retaining an environmental dimension within the programme for all pupils up to sixteen. Expansion of the core may well be accompanied by the elimination of options as courses cease to be viable, no longer justifying the allocation of resources (from teacher-hours to examination entry fees). All this might well redraw the curriculum map to the benefit of geography as a subject. In the last two decades a range of factors—

new degree courses at universities, new styles of teacher-training, more accessible legitimization procedures (e.g. CSE Mode 3), more liberal examining structures, new areas of public concern, and above all an expansionist context in terms of pupil numbers if not resources—have generated a degree of curriculum congestion in the broad area of the humanities. In some schools the secret garden of the curriculum has acquired attributes more characteristic of a tropical rain forest, as exotic plants—community studies, world studies, environmental studies, urban studies, social education—strive for a place in the sun. The pace of innovation, though more apparent than actual in terms of course content and teaching styles, has tended to reduce the legibility of the curriculum to the consumers of the education service. Arguably this has contributed, together with an inflated rhetoric of aims and objectives, to the widely acknowledged mood of public scepticism about education.

Geography teachers often feel frustrated and constrained by the persistent lay perception of the subject as the provision of locational and descriptive information about places, a perception shared by parents and colleagues: 'fact-based subjects like geography . . . are easily teachable and easily examinable. Their teaching and learning calls for no exceptional efforts on the part of teacher or pupil, just a relentless process of fact absorption.'[3] However, in the emerging curriculum politics of the 1980s, geographers might even come to value the fact that the subject at least possesses a public image. However mistakenly, the public thinks it knows what school geography is about—it would like pupils to know where things are, what places are like, and even how places come to be as they are. Similarly, the public believes that history is about the past, English is about fluency in reading and writing, and so on. In the tabloid terminology of back to basics, geography certainly sounds more like a basic than, say, community studies. The demographic context has certainly impinged upon curriculum debate in the last few years. It is now quite rare for those advocating any form of curriculum change or renewal to present an argument in terms of the establishment of a new subject with its attendant apparatus of textbooks, examinations, and subject associations. Too frequently such advocacy—of political education, of development studies, of environmental awareness—has not felt any obligation to examine the current content and approach within school geography, preferring to operate with the simple stereotype indicated above.

The new conventional wisdom—perhaps influenced by Bullock's *Language across the Curriculum* and the 'areas of experience' identified in the HMI Red Paper[4]—seems to be to recognize or develop the desired dimension (e.g. global, multicultural, political, environmental) within the existing curriculum map, rather than to attempt to establish wholly new territories.

Mixed ability and key ideas

Though the logistical constraints, leading to an expansion of the curriculum core, a thinning-out of the options jungle, and a moratorium on new subjects, may operate to strengthen geography's position, falling rolls have other less helpful implications. Though the subject may be taught to classes with a wide range of ability in the lower school, the differentiation of public examination targets generally makes a degree of ability-grouping necessary in the upper school. This is already a major headache for many departments faced with a wide range of available GCE and CSE syllabuses, exhibiting great disparities in prescribed course content and examination structure. Again, institutional rather than ideological imperatives will mean the persistence of mixed ability teaching into more upper school classes where there are insufficient candidates to establish separate GCE and CSE groups. Heads are often unsympathetic to arguments for small separate groups based upon the incompatibility of syllabuses so that, at least to 1985, there will be a premium upon ingenuity of teaching styles. If this means more individual and group work within the class, then a virtue may even be attained from this necessity.

These logistical considerations may also hasten the adoption of conceptually-based courses of the kind advocated in *The Teaching of Ideas in Geography*.[5] Indeed, one of the most interesting questions for the 1980s will concern the ability of teachers and pupils to cope with courses whose building-blocks are key ideas rather than areally defined quantities of information. It has been argued that an examining board which replaces 'the iron and steel industry in North East England' as a syllabus topic with 'the changing significance of factors affecting the location of manufacturing industry' is overestimating the ability of the teacher to select teaching content appropriate to the generalization. More significantly, it is maintained that pupils of average ability and below will experience difficulty in coping with questions or assignments which do not contain a specific locational trigger but merely invite candidates to write with reference to any area or location they have studied. Despite these misgivings, there can be no doubt than an ideas-based syllabus, whatever its intellectual and pedagogical rationale, will at least help geography teachers to overcome the increasingly tiresome coverage incompatibilities of most GCE and CSE syllabuses.

In surveying the future of school geography I make no apology for this emphasis upon dull and gritty management questions, for the context within which geography teachers operate is at least as significant as the shifting paradigms within the subject. Thus whilst many teachers have adopted the Schools Council Avery Hill 14–16 Project (perhaps we can leave the albatross-like Geography for the Young School Leaver label behind in the 1970s) because it closely corresponds with their own view of the subject, some have undoubtedly been strongly influenced by the fact that it appears to afford the possibility of teaching CSE and GCE pupils together without loss of efficiency. These preoccupations may of course wither away in the 1980s with the advent of a common sixteen-plus examination, a consummation devoutly to be wished by most teachers of the subject.

New examinations

The later 1970s saw one significant attempt at curriculum reconstruction: an attempt to broaden the sixteen-plus programme, represented by the ill-fated

N and F proposals. Feasibility studies indicated that many pupils would opt to continue their geographical education if a more liberal choice of sixth-form studies were made available. The course of the N and F debate suggests that one should not be too sanguine about the swift and painless introduction of common examinations at sixteen. The formulation of GCSE schemes seems all too likely to repeat some of the more depressing features of the N and F arguments—notably the wilful ignoring of the real capabilities of much of the clientele. As early as 1975 a third of all sixth-form pupils were not taking any advanced level course, and nearly a third of those who took the normal three A levels failed to get more than one pass. Similarly, society's pre-occupation with certification at sixteen is all too likely to ignore the needs of those pupils for whom formal public examinations will remain irrelevant, thus precluding the design of effective teaching and learning experiences for this group. As in the N and F sample syllabuses, we are likely to see again the growth of syllabuses by accretion, a process described thus by David Hall: 'Subject specialists . . . not only bring to panel discussions their own prefer-ences but recognize the validity of other perspectives. As reasonable men, they are prepared to include other themes in the syllabus, provided that their own persuasion is added to the inventory.'[6]

It seems extremely unlikely that the grip of the formal public examination system will be loosened during the 1980s. Recognizing this, curriculum development teams (such as the Schools Council Geography 16–19 Project team led by Michael Naish) have sought early legitimization through an examinations board, and have attempted to use the examination as an agent of change. Geographers in the schools are still attempting to digest the redefinition of their subject represented by recent major changes in Advanced level GCE syllabuses, and throughout the 1980s examinations are likely to be innovative rather than fossilizing. The problem remains that innovation has rarely been accompanied by sufficiently ruthless pruning of the syllabus. In the 1980s it may become increasingly difficult to defend fossilized teaching by reference to inert and unimaginative examination syllabuses. However, the overcrowded syllabus, with its inevitable concomitants of hectic pace, didactic exposition, and passive learning, will remain the major obstacle to more participative styles of work. When geographers claim that they would like to develop more resource-based independent learning, more games and simulations, more open-ended debate, more exploration of topical environ-mental issues on a local or global scale, but that they are prevented by the exigencies of coverage, they are not necessarily indulging in simple scapegoating. It should be noted that the accretion mechanism described by Hall seems to operate just as powerfully when groups of teachers meet to plan a syllabus. In the 1980s I am afraid that we will continue to try to teach—and/or arrange for pupils to learn—too much.

Continuity and progression

Falling rolls present further implications for the teaching of geography in the 1980s. It is likely that fewer teachers will have the opportunity of sixth-form work. Advocates of 11–18 secondary education argue that the quality of work below sixteen will inevitably suffer if teachers are deprived of the intellectual stimulus of work with older pupils, but very small sixth-form groups are hard to justify in educational, as well as economic terms. Recent curriculum change in geography has often had the unintended effect of obscuring or reducing continuity and progression within the subject. Thus the first three years may be regionally organized, employing an essentially descriptive, taxonomic paradigm (savanna grasslands etc.). The pupil, opting for the subject in year four because it stimulated his global curiosity in year three, may then encounter the issues-based, locality-emphasizing brand of geography provided in the Avery Hill Project, operating within a social science paradigm. Pursuing the subject beyond sixteen, the pupil is likely to encounter another methodological unconformity as he starts a systems-based Advanced level syllabus. Perhaps by 1990 continuity will be restored, but in the meantime the fragmentation of sixth-form geography teaching, partly due to syllabus demands but also in order to accommodate the several teachers who may demand a share in such work, provides an instance of the tension between professional and consumer interests.

If fewer geographers will have the opportunity of sixth-form work, more non-geographers will have the opportunity to try their hand at teaching the subject in the 1980s. It is likely to be more common to find the efforts of one or two specialist geographers supplemented by contributions from the deputy head, a physical education teacher, an historian, and so on. This again has implications for the geography curriculum; the leadership and organizational skills of the departmental head become vitally significant and such a situation is likely to involve the development of a fairly tightly structured course, possibly based firmly upon a textbook sequence, if the subject is to retain its identity.

Economic constraints

Falling rolls will be paralleled by economic constraints. It may prove difficult to sustain the fieldwork programmes that have become so central to good geography teaching. Perhaps this will be one area where we can be grateful for the public obsession with examinations, since the fieldwork requirement, as legitimized by the boards, will be easier to press upon reluctant Heads and administrators. If economic constraints have the effect of reducing the pressures on Swanage, Malham, etc., and of increasing the use of the immediate locality, particularly in urban environments, then they may not be wholly negative in their impact. Similarly, if economic constraints prompt a rather more judicious deployment of duplicated material, this might have a positive effect on teaching styles. In the next decade it may prove difficult, for economic reasons, to sustain and develop those groupings and networks of teachers that are such a key element in genuine curriculum change, as evidenced in all three Schools Council projects. Yet the isolation of teachers in small departmental teams, the scarcity of opportunities for teaching older pupils, the reduced intake of young teachers with new ideas—all these factors make such communication even more important. In-service support has a significant role to play, but it is not unduly cynical, I think, to see a broad relationship between in-service involvement and perceptions of personal career development. Again the basic demographic context of the 1980s is unhelpful, with greatly reduced opportunities for professional movement.

Curriculum convergence

Discussion of optimum curriculum content, and concern about the location of ultimate decision-making powers in this field, will no doubt continue into the 1980s, displaying all the characteristics of an essentially ersatz debate. On the one hand, the schools will be represented as beyond society's control, the private domain of power-hungry professionals who subject their charges to a self-indulgent and unwholesome diet, resulting in intellectual malnutrition and/or ideological indoctrination. On the other hand, there will be shrill declarations of resistance to interference by politicians and other unqualified persons, and allegations of a monstrous plot to subject all our children to an austere and colourless standard programme devised by DES bureaucrats. Both extremes will continue to construct imaginary opponents in order to have the satisfaction of demolishing them. Meanwhile, empirical studies such as the HMI Primary and Secondary Surveys demonstrate that the apparent autonomy of individual teachers and schools does not preclude a massive convergence of content and practice. The Primary Survey[7] unsurprisingly established that primary schools do in fact devote most of their time to basic communication skills, especially literacy and numeracy. The most effective schools, however, were those where content-free skill-practising did not dominate, but where a broad curriculum (including environmental study of all kinds) was maintained. The conclusion surely has significance for the secondary curriculum: pupils most want to read, write, speak, argue, calculate, *about* something. They cannot develop these skills in a vacuum, but need to employ them to cope with real problems. Good geographical teaching, with its skilful presentation of real-world questions (where should the hypermarket be sited? how are the costs and benefits distributed?), should provide a highly motivating context for the development of such skills.

Curriculum convergence is equally apparent in the secondary sector. For example, without any edict from any central authority, most geography teachers seem to have decided that pupils should not complete their compulsory geography course (often, regrettably, at fourteen) without an introduction to welfare geography on a global scale. Hence most third-year courses attempt to focus upon the contrasts and connections between North and South. Perhaps the most dramatic instances of curriculum convergence are to be found in lower school integrated schemes. The course documentation for such schemes generally places great emphasis upon the unique characteristics of the school, the area, the clientele, etc., no existing published resources having been found to be appropriate, and so on. And it is true that the staff involved have indeed invented their integrated programme from scratch. Yet the most casual examination of a collection of such schemes shows them to be remarkably similar. Indeed, were the syllabus to be prescribed by some authoritarian commissariat, I doubt if Early Man could improve on his remarkable predominance.

Integrated studies

The future of integrated or interdisciplinary schemes involving geography is problematical, lying in one of the cloudier sectors of my crystal ball. The current evidence is contradictory. If there is a degree of disenchantment, with some of the more grandiose schemes being dismantled or reduced in scope, many well-established lower-school foundation programmes continue to flourish, and fresh interdisciplinary initiatives continue to evolve. It is possible to discern a sort of constructive tension in this area. Many experienced teachers with departmental or institutional responsibilities have acquired a healthy scepticism about the sort of resounding rhetoric that tends to be associated with integrated studies. Such reservations are reinforced by recent attempts to sharpen the distinctive conceptual structures of contributory disciplines (symbolized by *The Teaching of Ideas in Geography*) and by the argument that public examination aspirations (still predominantly envisaged as subject success) are not best served by a less differentiated academic diet in the earlier years of secondary education. However, although the *ideological* impulse to integration (represented by such sentiments as 'the search for meaning in the curriculum finds its expression in the impulse towards integration . . . Integration is enshrined at the heart of contemporary progressive pedagogy')[8] may have lost some momentum, the logistical/ pastoral rationale remains strong. It is not necessary to invoke 'the seamless robe of knowledge' to justify a programme that enhances pupil security, minimizes pupil movement, and maximizes the effective use of scarce subject expertise.

The debate about subject integration, which will surely continue into the 1980s, can be peculiarly tedious and sterile. Discussions rapidly polarize around impossible stereotypes; vibrant, meaningful, relevant integrated teaching is contrasted with the dreary, rote-learning character of subject courses. Common sense suggests and observation confirms that neither structure has a monopoly of lively teaching strategies or mindless copying and colouring. Certainly such schemes place a premium upon the geographer's clarity of thought and expression: as Graves remarks, there is 'no great problem in incorporating a geographical element in a humanities course granted the geographer in the team knows what he wants to teach'.[9] There is room for improvement in geography's track-record here. Too often the geographical element seems to be little more than occasional work with maps, a device which confuses the study of the subject with the acquisition of tools for studying the subject. Essentially geographical questions relating to the character of places, spatial patterns, and networks are rarely central in such programmes. Perhaps one reason for this is that the non-specialist draws upon a stock of general awareness that includes the Romans but not farming systems, the child chimney sweeps but not the weather map. Hence many integrated studies schemes are strongly chronological in emphasis.

Geography—core or periphery?

Integrated studies rarely extends beyond fourteen. Thereafter geography teachers will be immersed in a different discussion. It is a pity that this discussion is dominated by a core-periphery metaphor. For this model has threatening associations for geographers. In an urban context properties peripheral to the core are taken over by expanding core functions; in a Third World context it is notoriously difficult to attract investment away from the core. A recent sequence of pronouncements from the DES and from Her Majesty's Inspectorate has contained strikingly few references to geographical and environmental education, though a special case was made out for history to be part of the core in the HMI paper *A View of the Curriculum* in January 1980. In a paper submitted to the Geographical Association, Richard Daugherty argues that 'In spite of the disclaimers to the contrary it is hard to escape the conclusion that, simply through failing so often even to appear on the agenda for discussion, the claims of geography to an important place in the curriculum are being ignored.'[10] Not only is geography not finding a place on the curriculum agenda, it seems to have no place either in developments such as the work of the Assessment of Performance Unit, which may exert an indirect influence on the shape of any framework or core.

However, any examination of actual practice in the schools (as described, for instance, in the HMI Secondary Survey) suggests that the subject is in little danger of imminent exclusion from the education of young Britons. The novelty of curriculum pronouncements from the centre is wearing off, and there are signs that diminishing returns are setting in as discussion papers, green, white and red, flutter down from on high. Though the slighter, blander documents (such as the DES *Framework for the School Curriculum* of January 1980) can be unhelpful as deployed by harassed head teachers or enthusiastic governors, it is possible to assemble support from equally authoritative sources. In 1974 the UK was a signatory to the UNESCO *Recommendations on Education for International Understanding*. According to this document, amongst the 'objectives to be regarded as major guiding principles of educational policy' should be 'an international dimension and a global perspective in education at all levels and in all its forms' and 'an awareness of the increasing global interdependence between peoples and nations'. The government circulated this document to all local education authorities in 1976. A year later a DES Green Paper on the curriculum contained the following observations: 'Nor are our young people sufficiently aware of the international interdependence of modern countries. Many of our most pressing international problems can only be solved internationally, for instance, environmental pollution; so our children need to be educated in international understanding as well. . . . Our society is a multicultural, multiracial one, and the curriculum should reflect a sympathetic understanding of the different cultures and races that now make up our society. . . . The curriculum should . . . reflect our need to know about and understand other countries.'[11]

A subject of public interest

I believe that geography will retain its important place in the curriculum throughout the 1980s, not because of official designations of any kind, but because it is concerned with an area of teaching and learning which corresponds with major public interests. After all, the emergence of the school subject in the late nineteenth century owed much to public enthusiasm for Empire: 'The colonies of England, her commerce, her emigrations, her wars, her missionaries, and her scientific explorers bring her into contact with all parts of the globe, and it is therefore a matter of imperial importance that no reasonable means should be neglected of training her youth in sound geographical knowledge.'[12] The popular climate for geographical education today is equally favourable, though for very different reasons.

Although there is an official climate of *laissez-faire* anti-planning so far as local and regional questions are concerned, there has been no detectable slowing in the massive growth of public interest in environmental matters, whether measured by media programming, publishing, adult education demands, or the growth of local amenity societies. The teaching themes and styles of the Avery Hill Project and its inventive examination papers are located at what should be an exciting interface between school geography and public environmental awareness. Just as in the 1880s parents and ratepayers felt that pupils should know something of the nature of the Empire, so in the 1980s most would support the idea that children should develop an informed and responsible attitude to environments—their own and other people's.

A similar gulf between official indifference and grassroots concern characterizes attitudes towards the geography of welfare on a global scale. The demand for materials, the interests of sixth-formers, the sales of the Brandt Report (which highlights the key role of education),[13] all indicate that the national mood is hardly as parochial as is sometimes alleged. Throughout the 1980s the activities of geography teachers should increasingly engage with these areas of broad popular concern.

Lessons from the new geography

If these opportunities are not taken up, and if geography in 1990 has become a marginal and neglected field of study in schools and colleges, it will assuredly *not* be because of governmental or LEA decrees or because of public antipathy; it will be because we have driven pupils away, largely through employing an unhelpful model in designing the secondary geography course. Something resembling a crude trickle-down model (long discredited in development economics) seems to have been adopted, in which the process of school curriculum change is broadly envisaged as an accelerating downward diffusion from higher education. It should not be necessary to reassert that school geography operates in a different context, with different functions: we must take care that the general educational values of the subject are not subverted by the assumed needs of a minority moving on to geography degree courses. In its more dehydrated forms nomothetic geography has had a disastrous effect on the subject as experienced by the ordinary pupil. Theory has not replaced traditional packets of information; it has *become* packets of information, with pupils copying out and learning the mystic shapes and terminologies of Christaller, Hoyt, von Thünen, and Rostow. In any case, it is surely hazardous to build the school geography curriculum upon something so essentially volatile as the university discipline. Other contributions to this book have documented the humanistic and radical critiques of the positivist geography, so unthinkingly adopted by adherents of the trickle-down model of curriculum change. Ironically, concern about the depredations of scientific geography at the school level is often most forcefully expressed by university geographers: 'So many of our models assume such things as isotropic plains, profit maximization, free markets, fair competition and, perhaps most important of all, an absence of secular progress; everything just happened overnight. But the world is not like that; people are not like that; the concept of original sin is undoubtedly much more important than that of satisficing man . . . So why bother school children with the rank-size rule, or any so-called laws of location; much more relevant is the basic political law—"get power and then hang on to it"—which has many spatial ramifications.'[14]

Significantly, this growing willingness to examine consumer perceptions, stimulated by the evident rejection of residual and reformed geography, is a characteristic of geographical-educational thinking in other countries. 'The problem is, therefore, not to forego the initiation into the world, the apprenticeship to environmental studies and geography, but instead of focusing it on a general presentation of civilization (history and geography apprehended at the level of the nations and the broader perspectives) it is preferable to see it as an apprenticeship to a personal exploration of the world. It is more important to develop an understanding of the forces and mechanisms at work in the world than to describe the great static configurations . . . there is the risk of breaking completely with the encyclopaedic education of yesteryear without replacing it by a working education adapted to real needs.'[15]

A priority for the future

Perhaps it is not so surprising that geographers in higher education should now be sounding the alarm about developments in school geography. There is now some evidence of the hazards involved in opening up too large a gulf between the natural interests, expectations and motivations of pupils, and what is offered in the school subject. As a percentage of the total entry, geography has claimed a smaller share of candidates at all levels—CSE, O level, and A level—since the mid 1970s. As a president of the Geographical Association pointed out, in commenting upon this 'slow but significant decline', this is to some extent 'an inevitable reaction to widening curriculum opportunity, but geography has fared worse than some cognate subjects at both 16+ and 18+ levels.'[16] When this trend is combined with the demographic context described earlier it is not surprising that academic geographers are becoming apprehensive about the supply of future undergraduates. A greater recognition of the need to take account of the professional expertise of the classroom geographer, to employ his familiarity with the abilities and interests of real pupils, should head the agenda for geographical education in the 1980s.

References

1   E. Briault and F. Smith, *Falling Rolls in Secondary Schools*, Part 1, (NFER Publishing Co., 1980).
2   *Aspects of Secondary Education in England* (HMSO, 1979).
3   Taken from an article on music education by Atarah Ben-Torim, *Guardian*, 9/1/81.
4   *Curriculum 11–16*, Working papers by HM Inspectorate (Department of Education and Science, 1977).
5   *The Teaching of Ideas in Geography*, HMI Series: Matters for Discussion 5 (HMSO, 1978).
6   D. Hall, *Geography and the Geography Teacher* (Unwin Education Books, 1976), p. 209.
7   *Primary Education in England* (HMSO, 1978).
8   G. Grace, *Teachers, Ideology and Control* (Routledge & Kegan Paul, 1978), p. 77.
9   N. J. Graves, *Curriculum Planning in Geography* (Heinemann, 1979), p. 86.
10 R. Daughtery, *The School Curriculum—an Emerging National Framework?* (1980)
11 *Education in Schools*, Green Paper (Department of Education and Science, 1977).
12 Royal Geographical Society, memorandum to the Vice-Chancellors of Oxford and Cambridge Universities, 1874; quoted in T. W. Freeman, *A History of Modern British Geography* (Longman, 1980), p. 35.
13 *North-South: a Programme for Survival* (Pan Books, 1980), p. 11.
14 R. J. Johnston, 'On geography and the organization of education', *Journal of Geography in Higher Education*, 1, 1 (1977), p. 7.
15 P. Claval, 'The aims of the teaching of geography in the second stage of French secondary education', in N. J. Graves (ed.), *Geographical Education: Curriculum Problems in certain European Countries with Special Reference to the 16–19 Age Group* (International Geographical Union Commission on Geographical Education, 1978), pp. 165–6.
16 J. A. Patmore, 'Geography and Relevance', *Geography*, 65, 4 (1980), pp. 167–8.

Chapter 14

The politics of school geography

John Huckle

What is the relationship between the changing geography curriculum in schools and economic and political change within society? How should geography teachers answer demands for a curriculum more relevant to the needs of industry? Is a common core curriculum, with or without geography, feasible and desirable? What is geography's contribution to secondary education? These are among the questions which this final chapter attempts to answer. To do so it places recent developments in school geography in the context of wider political debates about the nature and purpose of education, and provides theoretical support for the claim made in the introduction that much recent curriculum reform has served to alienate teachers and pupils and sustain the existing social order. It examines the claims made for geography in response to recent curriculum proposals and forecasts a period of conflict as progressive and radical teachers begin to introduce the approaches advocated elsewhere in this book.

Positivism—the new geography's hidden philosophy

If developments in geography and curriculum studies during the 1970s have taught us one thing, it is that no form of geography or schooling is politically neutral. The geographical facts and ideas which we teach our pupils shape their beliefs and attitudes concerning the world, while the activities and relationships we encourage in our classrooms affect their developing ability to participate in democratic social change. Our decisions about curriculum content and teaching methods are often subconscious and strongly influenced by textbook writers, examiners, curriculum experts, and colleagues, but they are inevitably moral and political choices with consequences for the lives of individuals and the future nature of society.

An exploration of the politics of the new geography in schools should begin by acknowledging its role in reinforcing positivism, a philosophy strongly identified with science. In the late 1960s academic geographers and curriculum theorists transformed the study of landscapes and education by adopting ideas and methods which more closely resembled those of the natural sciences. Their goal became the establishment of theory which could provide both more powerful forms of explanation and greater social recognition for their respective fields. While the type of theory and methodology developed in such areas of the natural sciences as physical geography was frequently their aim, their proposed reforms were generally undesirable and unrealistic. They often failed to appreciate the value assumptions inherent in positivist philosophy and the insurmountable difficulties of developing politically neutral theories to account for spatial and educational processes.

Positivism is a philosophy which regards knowledge as a given property of external reality amenable to study via value-free methods.[1] It has been successfully applied to physical geography where theories based on observation and experiment have greatly increased understanding of our surroundings. Explanation in geomorphology or meteorology is provided by networks of logically connected statements which have been rigorously tested and shown to have wide application. They are generally expressed in mathematical language and remain open to modification should the hypotheses they generate prove false when tested against reality. While such positivist theory represents an advance on many earlier accounts of the natural environment, it cannot be considered ethically neutral. Positivist physical geographers have consciously or subconsciously a view of the world which encourages people to manipulate and control their surroundings. It discounts human sensitivity and political commitment, and can provide no answers to questions about the ultimate meanings of life or nature. This is most dramatically illustrated by comparing their accounts of landscapes with those of poets and painters.

If positivists can provide only limited and biased explanations of natural phenomena, their ability to explain our social world is even more restricted. Claims to neutrality become even more suspect and the positivist theory offered to explain human landscapes and curricula fails to achieve the level of objectivity and reliability displayed by that in the natural sciences. There is no a priori reason why the phenomena of the social sciences should reward positivist theory building in the same way and their nature suggests that such attempts at explanation will be more prone to penetration by human values.

Although positivist theory provided the model or goal for those reforms in geography and education which prompted subsequent change in schools, the vast majority of the theories which appeared in the new textbooks and courses were normative in nature. Normative theory seeks to explain how landscapes and curricula should be organized and contains implicit value assumptions arising from the specific social and historical circumstances in which it developed. Unlike positivist theory, it can be verified by reference only to its own internal logic and not by examining the real world. In adopting normative theory to explain such phenomena as settlement patterns, industrial location, economic development, and curriculum planning, curriculum developers and teachers frequently failed to give sufficient attention to its ethical and political assumptions and to its limited power to explain current realities. Incorporated into curricula and taught in classrooms without reference to its origins and limitations, it appears as positivist theory and functions as ideology.[2] An uncritical introduction to such ideas as those of Christaller, Weber, Rostow, and Malthus encourages pupils to see their world in a particular and limited way and represents a deeply conservative education in which geography becomes an insidious form of social control. Presented as matter-of-fact explanations of settlements, factories, economies, and poverty, such ideas mask conflict in society and do little to encourage a search for alternative explanations based on different premises. Similar claims can be made about the curriculum theory on which the new geography was based. Here too a veneer of positivism frequently persuaded teachers to adopt methods of course planning which were not in their pupils' best interests.

Having suggested that the new geography strengthened an already powerful philosophy which encourages us to discount values, accept the world as given, and treat social issues as technical puzzles, it should be acknowledged that a more scientific school geography was not without its benefits and that few, if any, teachers accepted the new geography in a pure form. They generally incorporated new elements of positivist content and method alongside elements with other philosophical foundations, and the impact of new theoretical ideas was often substantially modified by curriculum developers and teachers as other contributors to this book have shown. Despite school geography's philosophical diversity and the often considerable gap between theory and practice, the new geography has become a powerful orthodoxy and there is a strong case for concern over its likely personal and social costs. While their extent and detail may occupy many writers in the 1980s, it is now necessary to examine the particular circumstances in which school geography was radically transformed.

School geography in a technocratic society

Although its nature and extent is usually problematic, there is a correspondence between curriculum change in schools and cultural and economic change within society. Schools and teachers do not exist in isolation and what happens in geography classrooms is to a considerable extent determined by prevailing forms of knowledge and social relationships in the world outside. The paths of influence between teachers and those with power in society are generally long and difficult to perceive, but geography lessons do play their part in ensuring that the state is supplied with workers and citizens who have appropriate knowledge, skills, values and attitudes. The reform of the geography curriculum in the 1970s should therefore be interpreted with reference to the political and educational climate of that time.[3]

The 1960s was an era of optimism based on technology. This was generally believed to be a self-directing force in society which would bring an unending range of benefits in its wake. The Labour Government which came to power in 1964 was firmly committed to this belief and regarded social justice as a by-product of technologically fuelled economic growth. If education could only provide school-leavers with the necessary skills, the economy would in turn provide the money for increased educational provision and greater equality of opportunity. Its social democratic beliefs regarded education as a self-evident 'good' and its policies were directed at increased provision and the removal of obstacles to the success of working-class pupils. Comprehensive schools, the raising of the leaving age, new forms of examination, the expansion of further and higher education, and a new attention to curriculum development were all outcomes of a policy which was to achieve only partial success since it largely overlooked the nature of the curriculum. It was in this setting that the new geography was born.

While politicians neglected curriculum content, it was no accident that the earliest curriculum development at the national level was in the field of science and that some geographers saw in positivism a means of enhancing the rigour and status of their subject. Geography as science was more in tune with the spirit of the times and more likely to gain a sympathetic ear when the head of geography was requesting increased timetable time or resources. Selective schools, producing future leaders and technocrats, played a key role in early reforms and many of their teachers saw in the new geography a means of furthering their own careers.

The more progressive teaching methods of the new geography may be seen as the product of demands for professionalism on the part of teachers, the changing labour needs of the economy, and the marketing of educational technology. During the late 1960s and early 1970s teachers felt themselves to be members of a threatened middle class whose income differentials over manual workers had narrowed considerably. Professionalism was a means of advancing and defending their relatively privileged position and, in retrospect, it may be suggested that curriculum development was the major activity upon which their growing claims were based. As they gained the initiative in the curriculum field, teachers not only seized upon positivist geography but were strongly influenced by the progressive methods being advocated in the still expanding colleges and departments of education. Through teacher education, curriculum development, and writing, the staff of these institutions modified the behaviour of pupils and teachers in many geography classrooms.

A greater attention to pupil-based learning and enquiry methods may also be interpreted as a response to the changing nature and number of jobs in an economy adapting to automation. The reformed classrooms were more like the work environment to be experienced by future technocrats, and so extended the range of abilities demanded that more subtle forms of grading and disciplining could operate. Failure could be attributed to an increased range of factors, while the school's newly acquired therapeutic function attempted to cope with feelings of personal failure by evoking psychological causes and created new career pathways for teachers in pastoral care. It can be argued that, as well as aiding professionalism and meeting the economy's changing labour requirements, the new geography sustained the profits of publishing houses and educational equipment manufacturers at a time when schools had money to spend.

In addition to more scientific content and progressive teaching methods, the new geography was justified in terms of rational curriculum theory of the behavioural-objectives type. An examination of the models and language which this employs suggests that it is an application of managerial methods designed to ensure efficiency and accountability. Behavioural objectives, a tendency to separate knowledge and values, and an apparent neglect of spontaneity and imagination render such curriculum specifications as new geography suitable instruments for those who wish to reproduce prevailing beliefs and patterns of social relations.[4] In geography rational curriculum theory was most strongly adopted by the departments and schools of education within the universities. It brought a new academic rigour to the study of geography in education, particularly when it was linked to psychological studies which promised greater efficiency in geographical learning, and an educational philosophy which served to justify the curriculum status quo.

This interpretation of the new geography as an adaptive response to a particular coalition of political, professional, and economic interests is subject to certain qualifications. First, as stated above, it is extremely unlikely that any one teacher or school department adopted positivist geography, progressive teaching methods, or rational curriculum planning in a pure form to the exclusion of other beliefs and practices. Secondly, the vast majority of teachers, including myself, were not conscious of the possible relationships between new geography and the wider society, some of which I have described. Such relationships were masked by the ideas and euphoria to be found in the books and journal articles of the time, and if school geography became a more willing servant of dominant interests, it was the result not of conspiracy but a lack of political awareness on the part of geography teachers. Subsequent developments in geography and curriculum studies exposed the weaknesses of positivism and provided teachers with new alternatives.

Alternatives to positivism

The alternative philosophies which attract geographers and curriculum theorists disenchanted with positivism offer the possibility of cultivating human sensitivity and creating a more just society. Of major significance as a humanistic alternative is phenomenology, an approach to reality which puts actual lived experience before abstract concepts and ideas. Phenomenology looks at things as they appear to us, as phenomena, and maintains that reality consists of subjective meanings within people's minds. These meanings constitute human consciousness which may be considered a social product since many of its elements are shared with others. Because meaning is the product of human interaction in specific social circumstances, there is no such thing as objective truth. Geography and curriculum are as they are because we see them as such and behave accordingly. Phenomenology removes the objective/subjective dichotomy and offers liberation from the restrictions of a scientific world view.

In curriculum studies phenomenology was adopted by those radical libertarians who developed the new, interpretive sociology of education.[5] This emphasized the relativity of school knowledge and began to examine the social processes whereby such phenomena as the new geography become established and legitimatized. Accounts of the social construction of educational knowledge in curriculum projects and classrooms challenged many existing orthodoxies and appeared to offer teachers the prospect of liberating pupils from imposed meanings. They provided a cultural rather than a political critique of existing curricula and prompted some to experiment with new forms of social studies in schools.[6]

Phenomenological insights lie at the heart of the humanistic geographical education discussed by John Fien in Chapter 4. By acknowledging everyday meanings of place and their role in cultivating self-awareness, it provides a valid means of enhancing developing human sensitivity. Humanistic geography lessons can provide a counter to the cold objectivity and universal meanings of new geography, but they may fail to take seriously the society external to the individual and those powerful political forces which limit human consciousness.

That phenomenology is an idealist counter to positivism which fails to give an adequate explanation of why certain meanings emerge and persist while others do not, is a belief which follows from the adoption of another philosophical alternative to positivism, Marxism. It suggests that the dominance of positivism must be countered at both the individual and community levels if we are to liberate human awareness and realize social justice. Consciousness, landscapes, and curricula are the products of material circumstances and a recognition that the new geography stifles pupils' sensitivity and supports the status quo should prompt geography teachers into political action to realize genuine alternatives. Marxists see much of the new geography as a form of ideology which serves advanced capitalism by instilling a depoliticized and consensus view of society.[7] Its ideas and activities are means of securing conformity to those beliefs and behaviours which sustain the existing social order and are, at the same time, instrumental in answering the labour needs of the economy.

As Ian Cook suggests in Chapter 7 a radical geographical education would reflect a conflict rather than a consensus view of society. It would explain human-environment relationships and patterns of spatial organization in terms of underlying political and economic realities and would explore the mounting problems of capitalism which affect pupils' lives. Lessons would reveal the social and historical origins of geographical ideas and would allow older pupils to debate openly alternative political and economic frameworks for society. Political education would be central to such a curriculum and teachers would seek a far greater degree of autonomy, answerable not to state bureaucrats but to the local community. A socialist approach to school geography is given greater attention later in this chapter for it enables teachers to face political realities and play a determining role in transforming an unjust society.[8]

Chapters 9 to 11 suggest that alternatives to positivism have had a greater influence on development and environmental education than they have had on the geographical mainstream. While geography teachers have perhaps been slow to introduce alternatives, it should be acknowledged that greater humanism and radicalism may not have the immediate appeal which was claimed by the new geography. Phenomenology and Marxism oppose dominant styles of thought and the introduction of humanistic and radical approaches is made more difficult by contemporary political realities.

The political climate changes

By the mid 1970s it was becoming clear to social democrats in the Labour

Party that their educational policies, designed to create a fairer and more prosperous society, were not working. By offering pupils of differing abilities widely different curricula, many comprehensive schools were continuing to reproduce inequality. There would need to be an extension of education policy into the area of the curriculum to ensure that all pupils were provided with a minimum common amount of useful knowledge. This shift of policy was also a response to a general loss of faith in education as growth in the economy came to an end and relative prosperity was replaced by inflation, recession, and growing unemployment.[9] Strong voices in the Great Debate, launched in 1976, alleged that schools were not sufficiently responsive to the needs of industry and sought a greater correspondence between schooling and the supposed manpower needs of industry. Social democrats now proposed greater state control over the curriculum and a greater role for Her Majesty's Inspectorate in monitoring and maintaining standards.

The discussion document *Curriculum 11–16*, which was written by Her Majesty's Inspectorate and published by the DES in 1977, envisaged a common element in all secondary curricula designed to introduce pupils to eight worthwhile areas of cultural experience. Its proposals were similar to those of certain curriculum theorists, who having recognized the political significance of curriculum content, now advocated a common curriculum as a means of realizing greater social justice.[10] The geography Inspectorate responded to *Curriculum 11–16* by suggesting that geography has a significant contribution to make in the areas of linguistic, social and political, ethical, mathematical and scientific experience. Their paper[11] had a strong positivist flavour and while it advocated a greater concern with social issues and decision-making, it set the debate in the context of personal values and attitudes rather than politics.

Once the Conservatives came to power in 1979, the political initiative in education shifted markedly to the right as monetarist policy demanded greater efficiency and accountability with decreased resources. Capitalism's dynamism was to be restored by a return to free market economics accompanied by a strong attack on the welfare state. Public education was to be trimmed of all waste and falling rolls used to justify a very real reduction in the quality of the service. The benevolent capitalism of social democrats was quickly transformed into a more divisive and oppressive system in which the school curriculum was to become an even more insidious form of social control. Progressive teachers were blamed for education's failure and there were strong demands for a return to traditional methods and a restoration of standards. Policy no longer made concessions to social justice and the curriculum proposed to provide the manpower needs of a revived economy was somewhat different from that outlined in *Curriculum 11–16*.

The consultative document *A Framework for the School Curriculum*, which the Department of Education and Science issued in 1980, envisaged a common core of subjects and stressed preparation for the adult world of work. English, mathematics, science, and modern languages make up the core and moral and social awareness are mentioned mainly in the context of religious education. The document's failure to recognize geography did not escape the attention of geographers,[12] but the prime value of the subject's apparent neglect is to remind us of the inevitably political nature of curriculum decisions.

While the DES proposed a core curriculum based on subjects supported by notions of minimum pupil competency and the assessment of performance, Her Majesty's Inspectorate and the Schools Council fought a defensive action on behalf of a common curriculum based on areas of experience. The Schools Council's 1981 Working Paper, *The Practical Curriculum*, bases its claims on an analysis of those kinds of experience, modes of teaching and learning, values and attitudes, and skills which all schools should encourage. It provided some of the background to the Schools Council Geography Committee's report *The Potential Contribution of Geography to the Education of Young People* which again made extensive claims on behalf of the subject. As with the earlier document from the geography Inspectorate, there was a strong flavour of positivism and a readiness to seek educational objectives within a particular view of the subject rather than from an analysis of the needs of pupils and society. Several sections of the report reflect a consensus and technocratic view of society and a limited awareness of the scope for political education in geography classrooms.

Similar criticisms may be made of three sets of 16-plus proposals for geography issued by a Working Party of the Schools Council Committee, the Joint Council of Examination Boards, and the Geographical Association's Working Party on Examinations in 1981/2. At first reading the suggested criteria for a single system of examining appear to offer clear procedures for rational curriculum construction even though there is limited advice as to what content or teaching strategies should result. Closer examination, however, suggests that their proposed criteria are cast within particular views of geography and society, and designed to further legitimate current 'good' practice. The criteria devalue pupils' lived experience of their environment, divorce spatial form from social process, and encourage the description and acceptance of spatial inequalities rather than their explanation and transformation. Social democratic bias is reflected in the visions of the future which the reports describe and in their readiness to refer to values rather than politics, environmental decisions rather than social choices, and social change rather than political struggle. While the Government restructured the Schools Council and cast strong doubts on plans for a joint 16-plus examination in the spring of 1982, the strongest voices in the preceding curriculum debate had clearly sought to place geography teachers firmly within a revised social democratic tradition.

The inherent weakness of this position is that it gives to education an ameliorative function which it cannot fulfil unless there is also change in patterns of property and power distribution outside schools. Curriculum proposals designed to increase social justice should stem from more general theories about the nature and causes of inequality in society. Educational action for justice cannot be divorced from political action elsewhere.

Towards a socialist approach to school geography

Like the members of the Social Democratic Party which emerged in 1981, social democrats in education favour consensus and co-operation rather than conflict and struggle. They believe that education can become a site for national, cultural, and political reconciliation and suggest that all fair-minded and reasonable people will see the virtue of a common curriculum which results from debate between teachers, the community, and the state. Such thinking fails to recognize the divided nature of society, the unequal access to power, and the manner in which the state now supports capital especially in times of crisis. Educational institutions cannot readily be adapted to the needs of the underprivileged, and in a divided society a common curriculum can rapidly become a new form of social control maintaining the existing order. Social democrats fail to derive common curriculum content from an analysis of class and society, but retreat to such conservative perspectives as Hirst's forms of knowledge. Their curriculum would have the effect of elevating the cultural meanings of particular groups, including groups of geographers, to the status of universals and would continue to favour those pupils who bring relevant cultural capital to school.[13]

A genuinely socialist approach to geography in schools should stem from a recognition that education is a means of both reproducing and challenging existing social and human-environment relations. Geography lessons can not only sustain prevailing beliefs and attitudes but may also allow pupils and teachers to examine alternatives openly and critically. There is scope for committed work within schools and the current crisis of capitalism provides geography teachers with significant opportunities. They teach about industry, towns, developing countries, resources, pollution, and world trade and are therefore well placed to explore the mounting contradictions of a mode of economic and social organization based on inequality and exploitation. By dealing with unemployment, inner city decay, underdevelopment, resource depletion, environmental deterioration, and the global economic order in a manner which acknowledges conflict and seeks political literacy, they are more likely to counter the apathy, indiscipline and truancy with which pupils currently register their discontent. Such work would represent an attempt to break the prevailing correspondence between schooling, culture, and economy and requires politically aware geography teachers who recognize their role as agents of social change.

In selecting curriculum content, socialist teachers should acknowledge cultural bias in society and the wide range of philosophies now reflected in geographical knowledge. These have varying potentials to meet human and social needs and we should be suspicious of any attempt to define the curriculum in terms of restricted or purely established views of the subject. Earlier chapters have suggested that rediscovered or emerging geographies now allow content which better answers personal and community needs and have also pointed to reformed methods in the classroom.

A curriculum which seeks to erode the hold of ideology over pupils' lives should also seek to challenge the exploitive social relations which characterize our society. Progressive teachers have done much to change the conditions in which knowledge is produced in schools and geographers would do well to adopt their collaborative, enquiry-based methods if they have not done so already. Experiential learning is central to education for justice, but we should be alert to the idealism of many progressivists. Their methods generally create more humane classrooms, but they are often politically naive and fail to cultivate the means whereby pupils can both understand and confront political power. The approaches of humanistic and radical geographical educators are complementary and the type of classroom activities being proposed in development and political education now allow geography teachers to overcome the weaknesses of an unpoliticized progressivism.

Implementing a socialist approach to geography in schools will not be easy. Teachers will attract charges of indoctrination and meet much opposition from those whose status and identity derive from prevailing definitions of geographical education. In the ensuing debates they will need not only the theoretical support which a growing literature offers,[14] but the skill to reveal the political nature of existing curricula. Colleagues will need to be persuaded of the inevitability of political education when teaching the social sciences and to be convinced that the adoption of a true socialist approach actually rules out indoctrination in the classroom. A more just and caring society can only be achieved by methods which reflect justice and tolerance and foster personal autonomy. Committed and responsible geography teachers are preferable to those who claim neutrality for a curriculum which uncritically supports the existing social order.

Commitment not only means a revised approach to curriculum and colleagues, but also requires teachers to take account of political debate outside school and seek support from those of similar persuasion. Socialist teachers can gain help from some parents, community groups, and other workers and these people's concerns and aspirations should continually modify the teachers' thinking about what happens in the classroom. Participation in politics and community maintains a freshness of approach and sustains the teacher's defences against those who continually threaten to accommodate new curriculum content and methods to established interests. The next stage in the development of school geography is likely to be one in which the intellectual and professional resources of radical teachers are tested to the full.

The future

The 1980s present geography teachers with a clear choice. They can further adapt their curriculum to prevailing conceptions of economy and society or they can make a constructive response to personal and social needs based on new philosophies in geography and curriculum studies. Those who opt for the latter face difficult but exciting times. They will need to make use of journals, in-service courses, conferences, and examinations to challenge current orthodoxies and to outline alternatives. They will need to read and produce more of the type of literature this book contains, generate new curriculum materials, and forge links in new directions. Above all, they will need to help each other experiment with more humanistic and radical class-rooms in order to test and modify their ideas in action. A decade of curriculum reform in geography has provided mechanisms for further change and current political and economic realities provide teachers with significant opportunities to exploit. It now remains to be seen whether these can be used to create a growing number of reflective and active geographers in our schools. As they begin to act on the suggestions contained in this book, school geography could begin to play a significant role in creating more fulfilled and happy individuals in a fairer and less troubled world. That surely is what school geography should be all about.

References

1   A clear account of positivism and alternative philosophies in geography is to be found in:
    M. E. Harvey and B. P. Holly (eds.), *Themes in Geographic Thought* (Croom Helm, 1981).
    Among those to review their impact on school geography have been:
    J. Wolforth, 'The new geography—and after?', *Geography*, 61, 3 (1976).
    P. T. Newby, 'The benefits and costs of the quantitative revolution', *Geography*, 65, 1 (1980).
2   For a discussion of ideology posing as science see:
    J. Larrain, *The Concept of Ideology* (Hutchinson, 1979).
    D. Gregory, *Ideology, Science and Human Geography* (Hutchinson, 1978).
3   This interpretative account of the new geography owes much to:
    D. Finn, R. Grant and R. Johnson, 'Social democracy, education and the crisis', in *On Ideology* (Centre for Contemporary Cultural Studies/Hutchinson, 1978).
    E. Benton, 'Education and politics', in *Education or Domination* (Arrow Books, 1974).
    R. Lee, 'The ivory tower, the blackboard jungle and the corporate state; a provocation on teaching progress in geography', in *Change and Tradition* (Queen Mary College, London, 1977).
4   Critiques of rational curriculum planning can be found in:
    F. Inglis, *Ideology and Imagination* (CUP, 1975).
    W. A. Reid, *Thinking about the Curriculum* (Routledge & Kegan Paul, 1978).
5   For an introduction to phenomenological and Marxist approaches in curriculum studies see:
    M. Sarup, *Marxism and Education* (Routledge & Kegan Paul, 1978).
6   G. Whitty, 'Sociology and the problem of radical education', in
    M. Flude and J. Ahier (eds.), *Educability, Schools and Ideology* (Croom Helm, 1974).
7   The role of the school curriculum in fostering a conservative perspective on society is discussed by:
    M. Apple, *Ideology and the Curriculum* (Routledge & Kegan Paul, 1979).

G. Whitty, 'Studying society: for social change or social control?', in G. Whitty and M. Young (eds.), *Explorations in the Politics of School Knowledge* (Nafferton, 1976).

8   Notions of social reconstruction via education are central to:
A. Curle, *Education for Liberation* (John Wiley, 1973).
B. Wren, *Education for Justice* (SCM Press, 1977).
K. Lynch, *Education for Community* (Macmillan, 1979).

9   For a popular introduction to the related crises of capitalism and education see:
R. Lekachman and B. Van Loon, *Capitalism for Beginners* (Writers and Readers, 1981).
Big Flame Teachers Commission, *The Crisis of Education* (Liverpool, 1977).
A more academic treatment is provided by:
M. Young and G. Whitty (eds.), *Society, State and Schooling* (The Falmar Press, 1977).
R. Dale, *et al.* (eds.), *Schooling and Capitalism* (Routledge & Kegan Paul, 1976).

10   D. Lawton, *Education and Social Justice* (Sage Publications, 1977).

11   Her Majesty's Inspectorate discussion paper, 'Geography in the school curriculum', *Teaching Geography* (Nov. 1978).

12   R. Daugherty and R. Walford, 'Government proposals for the school curriculum in England and Wales', *Geography*, 65, 3 (1980).
R. Daugherty, 'Geography and the school curriculum debate', in R. Walford (ed.), *Signposts for Geography Teaching* (Longman, 1981).

13   G. Whitty, 'Curriculum studies: a critique of some recent British orthodoxies', in M. Lawn and L. Barton (eds.), *Rethinking Curriculum Studies* (Croom Helm, 1981).

14   Continuing discussion of humanistic and radical approaches in geography and curriculum studies can be found in:
D. Stoddart (ed.), *Geography, Ideology and Social Concern* (Blackwell, 1981).
L. Barton, R. Meighan and S. Walker (eds.), *Schooling, Ideology and the Curriculum* (The Falmar Press, 1980).

Contributors

John Bale	*Lecturer in Department of Education, University of Keele*
Rex Beddis	*Senior adviser, humanities, Avon*
Eric Brough	*A Bedfordshire geography teacher*
Ian Cook	*Senior lecturer in geography, Liverpool Polytechnic*
John Fien	*Lecturer in geographical education, Brisbane College of Advanced Education, Kelvin Grove, Australia*
Nicholas Helburn	*Professor of geography, University of Colorado, Boulder, USA*
David Hicks	*Director, Centre for Peace Studies, St Martin's College, Lancaster*
John Huckle	*Head of geography, Bedford College of Higher Education*
Robin Richardson	*Adviser for multi-cultural education, Berkshire*
Frances Slater	*Senior lecturer in education, University of London Institute of Education*
Michael Storm	*Staff inspector for geography and environmental studies, Inner London Education Authority*
Chris Webb	*Director, Notting Dale Urban Studies Centre*

Index

aesthetic education, 58
anarchism, 76, 102
Art and the Built Environment Project, 17, 63, 105–6
art in the geography classroom, 59–61
Avery Hill 14–16 (GYSL) Project, 15, 27, 76, 134, 140

behavioural geography, 30–41, 43

capitalism, 77, 79, 102, 103, 149
case studies, 11, 83, 95
cognitive/mental maps, 33, 38–9
colonialism, 90, 140
confluent education, 49–54
core curriculum, 132, 139
curriculum development, 20, 47, 146, 153
curriculum rationalization, 132–3

Department of Education and Science, 17, 82, 139, 149
development, 91
development education, 89–93, 95–7

educational ideologies, 104
environmental competence, 46
environmental education, 99–110, 119
environmental ethics, 107–8
environmental ideologies, 100–3
examination, 12, 134–5, 142
experiential learning, 47, 152

falling rolls, 18, 134, 135
fieldwork, 12, 35–7, 61–2
14–18 (Bristol) Project, 15

Geographical Association, 107, 139, 141, 150
geography as science, 21, 30, 43, 146
geography and development education, 95–7
geography and environmental education, 106–7
Her Majesty's Inspectorate (HMI), 17, 132, 137, 149, 150
High School Geography Project, 13, 20–8
higher education, 18, 141
humanistic geography, 43–55
humanistic geographical education, 2–3
humanities, 44, 138

ideology, 4, 76, 104, 148

in-service education, 127–9, 137, 152
integrated studies, 4, 138

learner-centred approach, 47–9

Marxism, 75–6, 102, 148
mental/cognitive maps, 33, 38–9
mixed ability teaching, 133–4
models in geography, 14, 65
multi-ethnic/multi-cultural education, 93–5

neo-Marxism, 76
new geography, 1, 13–16, 64, 75, 140–1, 143–7
normative theory, 65, 144
Notting Dale Urban Studies Centre, 113–18
nuclear power, 86–7

perception, 32–5
perception studies and teaching, 35–41
phenomenology, 22, 147
physical geography, 144
place memory, 52
political education, 18, 66, 82–8, 110, 151–2
political literacy, 83–6
positivism, 22–3, 64, 143–5
private geography, 31–2, 45–6, 48
Programme for Political Education, 82–5, 87
progressive methods, 146, 152

racism, 90, 93
radical geography, 72, 74–81, 88
radical geographical education, 3–6
radicalism, 126–7
repertory grid, 39–41

Schools Council, 15, 150
semantic differential, 37
sixteen-plus proposals, 134, 150
16–19 Geography Project, 19, 27, 106, 135
socialist approach, 151–2
structured discussion exercises, 128–9

teaching skills, 125–6
teaching techniques, 51, 124–5
Third World, 60, 79, 89–93

urban studies, 112–20

values, 24, 33, 107, 126, 152
values education, 109

welfare approach, 64–73, 88
World Studies Project, 96, 131